MW00462750

MISSIONS UNMASKED

WHAT I NEVER KNEW ABOUT MISSIONARY LIFE

ADAM MOSLEY

Many of the names and situations in this book have been altered to protect the identities and ministries of those involved. Some stories are composites of multiple missionary experiences. However, all of the situations represented are real and are representative of the lives of many missionaries around the world.

THIS BOOK IS DEDICATED TO:

MELODY, MY INCREDIBLE WIFE AND
PARTNER IN ALL THESE CRAZY ADVENTURES

ALL OF MY MISSIONARY FRIENDS,
WITHOUT WHOM THESE LESSONS WOULD
HAVE NEVER BEEN LEARNED.

CONTENTS

INTRODUCTION

I WAS SEVEN YEARS old when my imagination was first captured by a visiting missionary. Margaret was a petite 40-something woman with fiery red hair to match her ferocious attitude. She had battled and defeated more personal and vocational demons than most people experience in a lifetime.

She was also a master storyteller. As I listened to Margaret recount the stories of her many years working with indigenous people in remote jungles, I was drawn into her fantastical world. This spiritual *Indiana Jones* spun harrowing tales that seemed specially-crafted for the mind of a second grade boy - full of mystery and intrigue, villains and heroes, a little bit of humor, and a healthy dose of the grotesque.

The movie *Goonies* had released that summer, and I remember thinking that Margaret's adventures sounded like a real life version of the adventures of Mouth, Mikey, Chunk, and the gang. Personally, I was a bit of a Chunk, but with Mikey aspirations, and Margaret gave me hope that people like me could live out wild adventures for God.

Three decades later, I still remember her dramatic tale of a battle with a tribal chief over the enslavement of neighboring villagers - one that saw her, at one point, facing the prospect of similar enslavement. I recall how she told, in another instance, of being forced to eat meat she knew to be undercooked (and the parasite she received in return for her cultural sensitivity). I was intrigued by Margaret. I thought I might be in love.

Looking back, I see that my tingly feelings weren't for Margaret at all, but rather, I had developed a series crush for missions

I didn't know it at the time, but I had been bitten by the *missions bug*. And like the parasite Margaret spoke of in such vivid detail, that little bug would lie dormant in me for years, only to reemerge with a vengeance when I least expected it.

IMMERSED IN MISSIONS

Growing up in a traditional evangelical church, I was inundated with missionaries and their causes for most of my life. Some of my most memorable Sunday nights were spent sitting on padded, burnt orange pews, listening to seasoned missionaries spin their tales of God-inspired adventure. I was wowed by the slideshows of exotic faraway lands and entranced by the stories of harrowing escapades.

The church where I grew up was a community that understood and embraced the importance of loving and serving people locally and globally. For well over a decade, we had a paper-covered bulletin board in our church lobby which was dedicated to global missions. On that bulletin board was a map of the world, with pushpins indicating each city and country where we were supporting missions efforts. Next to the pushpin was a picture of the individual or family, and a brief description of the work they were doing.

That board always fascinated me. As a kid growing up in a rural farming community, I couldn't imagine what life must be like in other parts of the world. There was something exciting and mysterious about it all. Of course, when I was in elementary school, my friends and I regularly moved those pushpins around, so it's hard to know where our missions partners actually were, but we knew there were people out there who were relying on our support to do great work in the world. Even as a kid, I knew this was important stuff.

My family was fully engaged in the missions activities of the church. We would periodically receive pictures and postcards from our missionary friends, and we eagerly awaited the moment the giant fundraising thermometer at the front of the church would finally reach its peak. (If we were really lucky, it would receive some additional red paint at the top, indicating that we had far surpassed our goal.)

We even had personal friends and prominent members of our church who left their careers and families behind to serve in the mission field. We sent people out to become bible translators and bush pilots in the far reaches of the world. Global missions had a significant impact on our lives and the lives of those in our church.

All of this missions activity was so normal in our social circles that it never occurred to me that others didn't have these kinds of experiences. In fact, it is only in writing this book that I've realized just how much I was immersed in missions at a young age.

FROM CAPTIVATED CHILD TO PRESUMPTIVE PASTOR

I grew up fast. At the age of 18, I was like most other kids my age - fascinated by the newfound freedom of college life, dreaming of my preferred future, and determined to "be my own man."

Just 18 months later, I was married and moving to Cincinnati to become Associate Pastor (read: glorified intern who could also play the guitar and sing) for a new suburban church plant. Adulthood came rushing in, and I never looked back.

As I took the speedy but bumpy path toward pastoral ministry, a few of my childhood friends went on to serve in some of the largest missions organizations in the world. In my new role and new city, I made new acquaintances who had spent a good portion of their lives in dangerous places. Even though we were safely tucked away in the American suburbs, many of my friends were sponsoring an impoverished child somewhere in the world, and they had the pictures and letters stuck to their refrigerator to prove it. I thought I had a pretty good grasp on this whole missions thing.

As the pages flipped on the calendar of my life, I settled into my pastoral vocation. Pastors, I discovered, are expected to be experts in anything and everything even remotely related to church, God, and faith - and to be honest, I learned to fake it pretty well.

In 2009, I joined the staff of a 7 year old church plant in suburban Houston, where I quickly took on the responsibility of overseeing the global missions efforts of the church. It was a small church, but we supported a couple of missionaries, and I was given the task of connecting with them, communicating with them, and providing some level of pastoral care and support.

I did what I could, with only a meager understanding of their world, to offer that support. I followed their progress and attempted to correspond with them regularly. If I received an urgent plea for help, I responded in whatever way I could as an individual, and got our church leaders and members involved when appropriate. I sought to invest in real relationships with these people who were half a world away, and I earnestly tried to involve them in the life of our church. I wanted to facilitate a dialogue - a two way discussion - rather than a one-way monologue of status updates and prayer requests.

I went on to form a missions task force at the church - a group designed to involve other church members in the missions process. I even convinced our church board to set aside money each month to create an emergency reserve to assist our missionaries in times of crisis. I was looked to as the de facto church missions expert. Of course, I liked to think it was because I really knew about missions. More likely, it was because I was a squeaky wheel advocating for global missions, even though I didn't know what I was doing.

A RE-EDUCATION

To be fair to myself, there were at least a few things I *did* know. I knew it was hard living in other cultures, learning other languages, and dealing with people who may not be thrilled that you're there. I knew it was tough to raise money for missions work. I knew there was more work to be done than people to do it. This was my starting point, and I used that knowledge to inform my interactions with missionaries.

There were also quite a few things I didn't know - many of which I would come to realize can only be learned by developing deep relationships with actual missionaries. It turns out there are aspects of missionary life that simply aren't advertised. The 30 minute fundraising presentations made in churches on Sundays are carefully curated snapshots of ministry. They are designed for maximum effect in a minimum amount of time - marketing pitches, not state-of-the-ministry addresses.

Now, let me be clear: there's nothing wrong with marketing, especially for a worthwhile cause. Part of the process of doing good work and inviting others into it is learning how to effectively communicate what you are doing and why others should join in. So, while these marketing pitches have their merit, they simply don't tell the whole story. They can't. Missionary life is too complex to be boiled down into a few slides and a video montage.

Not only that, but most missionaries don't want to share their whole life with the world any more than you or I. We all form some kind of line between private and public life, and for missionaries, that line tends to always be pushed toward the public end of the spectrum. To be a missionary is to live life in a fish bowl, and most missionaries do what they can, when they can, to avoid that feeling, not contribute to it.

In fact, because of the realities of life on the mission field, the majority of missionaries allow very few people see the full scope of their life and work. Even long-time, devoted supporters often have no idea of the everyday realities faced by their beneficiaries. The details and struggles of life don't get posted on the missions bulletin board (for good reason). Typically, only the closest friends and relatives have access to that world.

This is a book about that world. It's a world I am privileged to live in, due in part to my own curiosity, and in part to the great friends I've been entrusted with. You see, I don't think of myself as a missionary. I'm just a pastor who happens to serve in Kenya, rather than in Omaha or Tallahassee. And while some insist that my vocation and location make me a missionary, I always argue that my life is still, in many ways, very different from my missionary friends.

While we share some similarities, given our cross-cultural lifestyle and the God-centered nature of our work, there are also many missionary challenges I don't face. My challenges are different. My challenges are pastoral. And it is some of these pastoral challenges that have driven me to write this book, as an attempt to shed light on the often misunderstood life of a missionary.

PASTORAL CONFESSIONS

What follows, then, is a pastoral perspective on missionary life - a second-hand account of the realities on the ground. It's a collection of learnings resulting from conversations with people who have answered God's call to go into all the world, and in some cases, paid a hefty price for doing so. In the process of trying to figure out missions, I discovered - truly for the first time - the missionary. And I uncovered some foundational truths that completely changed my perception of missionary life.

When I sat down with missionaries, I learned to stop talking and start listening. I found that if I listened more intently and asked better questions, I could get beyond the newsletter updates and social media snippets. If I pressed in, I could get beneath the veneer to the vulnerable - to lift the unmask missions and the realities of missionary life.

Most importantly, in the midst of these conversations, I discovered I wasn't the only one who hadn't been listening. Many missionaries I spoke to felt like there was *no one* who understood them. In conversation after conversation, I found myself saying, "Oh, I've got a lot to learn." Indeed, *we* have a lot to learn.

As I began to contemplate how best to capture my learnings in written form, I decided to categorize them into a few groups:

First are the things I *thought* I knew. These are the areas where I had been operating under one set of assumptions, only to discover that I was either completely askew, or that there were factors I had failed to consider. These are the areas where I had to undo a lot of my thinking.

Second are the things I *knew* I didn't know. I was aware that there were parts of missions work and missionaries that I didn't understand. These are the areas where I sought to ask questions and get answers - things about which I was naturally inquisitive. Initially, this is the only area of my missions knowledge I was actively seeking to improve.

Then there's the last group - the things I *didn't know* I didn't know. The more I learn, the more I realize that this group is a vast and ever-expanding galaxy of information and experience. Every day I discover more items and questions to add to this group. What you find here are just a few insights. Tomorrow, I'll have more. And the next day. And the next.

Throughout my learning process, and in the midst of conversations with my missionary friends, I discovered how ignorant I was, and that I had failed in so many ways as a friend, pastor, and supporter of missionaries. I had allowed inference, intuition, and ignorance to drive my missions response, rather than investing in relationships and working to understand the situation at hand. Not only did I not understand missions, I didn't even have a *grid* for understanding. There was so much in my own mind that I had to deconstruct before I could begin to grasp the realities of this world.

This book, perhaps, is my attempt at a confession - the words of a contrite pastor committed to improving a poor track record. Maybe it's just an empathetic attempt at solidarity with my missionary friends. Ultimately, I hope it's much more than that. It is my prayer that this book will open the eyes of others who are trying their best to support, pastor, and befriend missionaries around the world.

If you picked up this book, you probably have, or desire to have, some involvement in global missions. Perhaps you are even considering becoming a missionary yourself, or you are a pastor or church leader looking to "send well." Whatever your particular situation, it is obvious that you care about missions, about missionaries, and about how best to go about God's work in the world. I want to encourage you and challenge you in the journey.

You don't have to reinvent the wheel. Please allow my mistakes and the mistakes of others to inform your decisions, deepen your conversations, and bring hope to the incredible missionaries in your life. They deserve nothing less.

WHAT I THOUGHT I KNEW

WHAT DOES IT TAKE for you to be convinced that you're wrong? Some people sputter through life consumed with the idea that they are *always* wrong, but for most of us, it takes some arm twisting. We assume that we're right, and it will take a mountain of evidence to prove otherwise. But there is an old saying about what happens when you assume (which I...ahem...assume you probably know) and I've had that truth smack me in the face repeatedly.

When I took on the role of Worship Pastor/Associate Pastor at the wise old age of 20, I began working in a full-time, though unpaid, capacity that served as my first exposure to the unique world of vocational ministry. I thought I was ready. Though I was young, I had prepared well for this new adventure. I read books, listened to lectures, and sought the wisdom of those who had gone before. If we were going to "do church," we were going to do it *right*.

I remember multi-hour conversations centered around the proper format for a weekend service, careful attention to the lighting, the seating, and even how we dressed. It was the late 90s, and all the experts had thoughts on just how to attract *Generation X*. And we listened to them all - never mind that many of them contradicted each other (or that some of them contradicted themselves.)

We also spent a great deal of time in prayer, which often served to contradict the so-called experts, but also to give us confidence in the direction we were heading. At the time, I was a little less into the prayer stuff, and a little more focused on the so-called *practical* side of the equation. Fortunately, we had others around us who maintained a high value for prayer.

By the time our team launched the church, I was a self-styled expert in church planting. I knew exactly how to attract a crowd of *unchurched* people, and if only everyone else would listen to me, we would have throngs of people filing into our new church each and every Sunday. That church planting effort eventually went south and was shuttered, though I still believe it was a valuable piece of the life puzzle for quite few of us.

After watching that young church fizzle, I took my expertise to another church - the largest in town. Bolstered by my church planting experience, in a way that only an arrogant know-it-all could be, I began inserting my "wisdom" into conversations with my new colleagues.

It would take several more years for me to realize that all my grand solutions weren't really all that grand.

THE FIXER

In my twenties, I thought I knew everything. I could come up with a solution to any problem, an answer for every question. I was smart and driven and mature beyond my years. If only someone would put me in charge - for a day, a week, a year - I could straighten this mess out. (This, I suspect is the motivation for many a Seminary pursuit or Political Science degree.)

For the young me, everything could be boiled down to some kind of simple equation. That equation could then be solved for x, and we could move on to the next problem. I fancied myself a bit of a fixer, if only people would listen. I had a lot of confidence in my own ideas and plans.

Over time, of course, I have learned that some things can't be boiled down so easily. Not everything fits the equation, and sometimes, even after a problem or question is reduced to its simplest form, it will still prove to be too complex or too cumbersome to easily solve.

As I dove headlong into understanding missions, I learned that there are assumptions I've made and myths I've believed that simply don't ring true. Whether due to naiveté, arrogance, or misinformation, this type of supposition can lead to confusion, isolation, and frustration for missionaries - those who have given their lives to battling the realities of a broken world, only to be offered pithy solutions by those who are supposed to understand.

Our assumptions, it turns out, guide and inform nearly everything we do in life, and when we are armed with incorrect assumptions, they can have a dramatic impact on our ability to do the work of God's Kingdom in the world. Assumptions about people, about organizations, and even about ourselves are like the current flowing under a mighty ship. Without recognition of the direction and strength of our assumptions, we can find ourselves adrift at sea - far off course - even in our most honest attempts to do good.

When I think back on some of my initial interactions with missionaries, I wince. When I recall the things I *thought,* but didn't say out loud, I bow in repentance. I didn't get it. I *thought* I knew, but I was clueless.

In face-to-face conversations, over the phone, through internet chat, and through social media, I see so many others making the same kind of mistakes I did - responding with either bumper sticker theology or cynicism to the real life and real challenges facing missionaries every day. Whether attempting to coddle, to inspire, or to challenge, our misguided attempts to be helpful often leave our missionary friends feeling abandoned, alone, and misunderstood.

When I look back at my former response to missionaries, I'm reminded of a friend who used to tell me, "Beware the new college graduate. They know everything, but they've done nothing." That was *me* when it came to missions work, and it describes so many others. You go on a two week missions trip and think you know it all. You talk to one family or one missionary, and you think you can "fix" them. If only someone would listen, you could get this sorted out.

Like the 20-something me, or the newly minted college graduate, many of us have a lot to learn and experience before we can be of any real help to our missionary friends. The truth is, none of us have it all figured out. All of us are still learning. My own understanding of missions, and respect for missionaries, is deepened with each conversation and broadened with each visit to a project site. I will never stop learning. I will never stop listening.

If we are to support missionaries well, we must seek first to understand, then to understand more. We have to be willing to accept the fact that sitting thousands of miles away, our five-minute solutions are useless. We have to know that only a life lived on the ground, among the people, can generate real answers.

LISTENING TO THE EXPERTS

Last week, my wife was watching a reality TV show where a bride-to-be goes shopping for her wedding dress. The whole point of the show is for the bride to find her "dream dress." Now, setting aside for a moment the fact that some of these dresses cost more than my first car, and that all too often, newlyweds and their parents are falling deep into debt to pull off extravagant weddings, there is a different lesson for us as we interact with missionaries.

As I watched this show, I realized that everyone thinks they are an expert when it comes to wedding dresses, except for the bride herself. Most of the women on the show bring an entourage of people with them - moms, aunts, sisters, and best friends - and the crowd of advisors always seems to think they know what the *perfect dress* is.

They'll talk about the fit, the flare, and the fashion as if they are regular columnists for Vogue. Sometimes they'll even give their credentials. "I'm a wedding photographer," they'll say. Or, "I've known Stacey her whole life, so I know what she likes." The entourage is confident in their ability to assess the dress. The bride is less so.

Most brides on the show are very unsure of what they are looking for. They might come in with an idea, but after trying on a few dresses, they are more confused than ever. Eventually, and sometimes to the chagrin of their entourage, these brides begin to lean on the opinion of the trained and seasoned consultants in the boutique - people who *actually* know about dresses - whose wisdom goes beyond a few fashion industry buzzwords. Years of first-hand experience, it turns out, is more beneficial than made-up-on-the-spot opinions.

Those of us who are trying in earnest to support missionaries too often find ourselves in the role of the bride. We bring our own assumptions to the room, and quickly become uneasy about them. Meanwhile, the people in our entourage - our co-workers, church members, elder board, etc. - are shouting us down with their strong opinions and reminding us of their credentials.

But who is the expert? Who is the one person who truly knows about missions work? Is it the person who goes on a missions trip once a year, or the person who lives 365 days a year in a war-torn country? Is it the one who sponsors an impoverished child to go to school, or the one who provides daily care for a dozen orphaned children in some of the world's harshest conditions?

It's time we look to the experts - the missionaries

themselves. Even missions veterans have to accept that many of our old paradigms are no longer valid. To return to the metaphor, the dress that worked 30 years ago might not work today. We have to recognize that even long-held missions protocol and methodology - used for decades by many multi-national missions organizations - is being challenged by new social and scientific insight into cross-cultural relations. Let us stop trying to be experts, and return to being students.

The things I thought I knew about missions have been upended by my conversations with missionary friends. *They* are the experts who are living this life on a daily basis. When I was willing to listen and dig into their encyclopedic knowledge, I discovered that many of my previous assumptions about missionary life were completely overturned by reality. In reading this book, perhaps some of your assumptions will be similarly challenged.

Maybe you'll be the bride who, after trying on a dozen dresses that fit her personal wish list (and that of her entourage), finally listens to the expert and discovers that the perfect fit has been hanging on the rack all along. I hope you're challenged. I hope you're inspired. I hope that, in the end, you are a better friend and supporter of your missionary partners because you are able let go of what you thought you knew and embrace the wisdom that can only come from the true experts.

THE MAKEUP OF A MISSIONARY

ONE OF THE FIRST missionaries I ever spent considerable time with was a bible translator for a large missions organization. Harold was an academic, with multiple degrees and the appropriate scholarly beard - a sage of scripture. This guy had forgotten more about the bible than I would ever learn. His astounding proficiency in languages ranged from ancient biblical to modern tribal and was unmatched by anyone I have met before or since.

Harold was a missionary's missionary. Not only did he study the bible academically, he lived and breathed its words. He was devoted to simple living, to serving the poor, and to the kind of personal and intimate prayer life that Jesus modeled, but few ever realize. Harold was the closest thing to a saint I think I've ever known. I assumed all missionaries were like Harold. They must be, right?

Over the years, I would meet a lot of missionaries who didn't match Harold's archetype. It turns out you don't have to have an awesome beard to be an awesome missionary. Still, I supposed that those missionaries I encountered were vastly more spiritual than I. Surely their days were filled with quiet times and bible studies, with psalms, hymns, and spiritual songs, with strength for today and bright hope for tomorrow. That, I reasoned, must be the kind of stuff hard-wired into a missionary. Surely that was built into the makeup of every single person called by God to go into all the world.

After all, missionaries are a unique breed. Normal people don't give up promising careers to go live in a developing nation. Average people don't move from Birmingham to Bangladesh to start an organization with almost no funding or prior experience. Missionaries, though, do these things as a matter of course. Stepping out in faith seems to be built into them, like breathing or eating. They are the great adventurers for God - trailblazing pioneers of the faith. And let's face it, they're pretty cool.

But if you ask most missionaries, whether well-disciplined quiet time aficionados or risk-taking thrill-seekers, they'll tell you that they are much more ordinary than they are extraordinary. Moving to a far away land does not automatically make you a spiritual person. Working with impoverished people doesn't make you a saint. Even struggling under the weight of oppression doesn't mold you into a paramour of prayer.

You see, the majority of missionaries I've encountered are not super-saints at all. They are just ordinary people who are trying their best to do what they've been created to do. They often feel unprepared spiritually, emotionally, and physically for the task at hand, and many question why God would call them to this task in the first place. Fortunately, they are in good company. The leaders of the first century church were in much the same boat.

JESUS KIND OF PEOPLE

As Jesus began his public ministry, he was faced with a choice. He could have gone into the synagogue and attempted to recruit the best and brightest. He could have gone after a young Saul, trained as a Pharisee, or recruited Joseph of Aramethea, one of the prominent members of the High Priest's Council. Indeed, these are people whose heart would eventually bend toward Jesus.

But in launching his ministry, Jesus chose a different type of person. The first he called were fishermen - blue collar laborers who understood the value of a hard day's work. They were gruff and surly - probably not the religious type. And when he invited them to come and follow - to join him in whatever he was about to do - they left behind their families, their jobs, their personal security, and the only life they had ever known.

These men, and eventually women, set out with Jesus on a fascinating journey that would be encouraging and inspiring, but also frustrating and challenging. Jesus' teaching would clarify many things for them, but in the end, they were probably left with more questions than answers. Ultimately, they were also left in charge of starting a new kind of church in the midst of a religious and political climate which had just resulted in the torture and death of their leader.

They weren't powerful or educated or politically-connected. They were ordinary. They were messed up. But they were willing.

Simon Peter, who would serve as a key leader for the emerging church of Jesus, was a fisherman who laid down his net and followed Jesus into the unknown. Matthew, who would go on to tell and retell the story of Jesus, was a corrupt government official before encountering the Savior of the world. Thomas doubted. Peter denied. John questioned. They were ordinary people walking out their calling in fallible human ways, but they changed the world forever.

Missionaries should take great comfort in knowing that God has, throughout history, shown a willingness and a proclivity to use ordinary people to do extraordinary things. Those of us who support missionaries should, I believe, adjust our expectations and recognize this truth. We should prepare ourselves for the realities of missionary life. We shouldn't bury our head in the sand and pretend that missionaries don't face difficulties, that marriages aren't in shambles, that kids don't rebel, and that ministry partners don't get irritated with each other.

Jesus, the greatest leader in the history of the world, invested heavily in a group of 12 guys for three years, yet they spent their last night with him arguing over their pecking order in his kingdom, quarreling over who would betray him, who would deny him, and who would defend him. Their human weakness was on full display in the upper room, in the Garden of Gethsemane, and in the High Priest's courtyard. Even so, Jesus, after his resurrection, would double down on his decision to use this team of regular people to change the world.

And he is still affirming that decision today. Sure, there are some extraordinary people who have been called into service in the Kingdom of God, but the majority, like the apostles before them, are overwhelmingly average. You see, I knew that missionaries did amazing work. What never fully grasped is that missionaries are just normal people like you and me.

THE ENDURING YES

Within the missionary community, you will find people who pray multiple times a day, and those who hardly remember to pray at all. There are some who rely on God for everything, and some who pour themselves into planning out every detail without even a nod toward the Almighty. Some spend their free time studying the bible, while others prefer to study reality TV.

They are single, married, divorced, and widowed. They're in shape and out of shape, and from every ethnic, cultural, economic, and family background imaginable. In short, the makeup of the missionary community is not that different than the makeup of the culture from which they came. My community of missionary friends doesn't really look all that different than my community of friends in the American suburbs. Sure, the details may differ, but the demographics don't. The vocations may vary, but the struggles are the same.

Some people might be appalled to learn that missionaries have the same hardships and hang-ups as the rest of us. We like to think that missionaries are something other than normal human beings. We want to hope that there is some differentiation between *us* and *them* - perhaps because we want to send God's best into the world, or perhaps because we want to ensure there's a gap between the *called* missionary and the *comfortable* me.

So, what *is* the makeup of a missionary? Of course,

obedience comes into play. God says to go, so they go. I've even met missionaries who didn't set out to be missionaries, but who obeyed God's calling to take a step into the unknown. For these folks, obedience was their key driver, especially in the beginning. Eventually, many of them have discovered the truth that obedience to God ultimately aligns us with his heart. It somehow changes us from the inside out, and causes God's desires to become our desires. Obedience, then, is a powerful force in the life of a missionary.

Tenacity also plays a big role. Missionaries are some of the most tenacious people I've ever met. They won't stop until they accomplish their goal. Forget for a moment about the many countries around the world where being a missionary for Jesus can get you arrested or killed. Even in more welcoming countries, missionary life is full of frustration, difficulty, and roadblocks. Let's face it, people who give up easily aren't typically a great fit for missionary work. Tenacity is in the job description.

But for me, there is no single word that is more important or all-encompassing for a missionary than this: *Yes*. A missionary is someone who says yes to God...and who keeps saying yes over and over, even in the face of tremendous difficulty. This is what I call the *enduring yes* of the missionary. People on a mission simply don't give up until the mission is accomplished. They keep fighting, keep hoping, keep believing in the God who sent them on this mission. They keep saying yes to the mission and to the God of the mission.

The Apostle Paul, arguably Christianity's first and most well-known missionary, expressed well the enduring yes of a missionary in his letter to the church at Corinth:

Five times I received from the Jews the forty lashes minus one. Three times I was beaten with rods, once I was pelted with stones, three times I was shipwrecked, I spent a night and a day in the open sea, I have been constantly on the move. I have been in danger from rivers, in danger from bandits, in danger from my fellow Jews, in danger from Gentiles; in danger in the city, in danger in the country, in danger at sea; and in danger from false believers. I have labored and toiled and have often gone without sleep; I have known hunger and thirst and have often gone without food; I have been cold and naked. Besides everything else, I face daily the pressure of my concern for all the churches. Who is weak, and I do not feel weak? Who is led into sin, and I do not inwardly burn?

2 Corinthians 11:24-29

Paul kept saying yes to God, even though he faced a laundry list of troubles. Every time he got knocked down, he found it in himself to get back up, dust himself off, and take another crack at it - to say yes to God once more. Some might look at Paul's struggles and say, "I could never be so strong," but Paul doesn't see it that way. In the very next verse, he says,

If I must boast, I will boast of the things that show my weakness.

2 Corinthians 11:30

Then, in chapter 12, he goes on to say,

That is why, for Christ's sake, I delight in weaknesses, in insults, in hardships, in persecutions, in difficulties. For when I am weak, then I am strong.

2 Corinthians 12:10

These are not the words of a titan of the faith proclaiming his superior spiritual might. These are the words of a missionary being real with the people he is leading. Yes, his life was hard and he persevered, but in the end, he was a weak man who recognized that only through his weakness could God really shine. Only when he reached the end of his abilities was he able to see just how capable God was of handling the situation.

Trust in God, hope for the future, and unrivaled determination may keep a missionary in the field through the tough times, but like Paul, it is in the moments of weakness that they truly see God work. Super-saints, I suppose, might not be so desperate. Normal people who know they're in over their heads, who recognize their own limitations, who know they've reached the end of their abilities - those people will cry out to God in their weakness and will be delighted to watch him move.

I thought I knew what made a missionary, but I've discovered that really, it just takes an *enduring yes*.

THE PURPOSE OF LONG-TERM MISSIONS

CHRISTINE IS A FORMER suburban school teacher turned missionary. A single female living as a leadership coach in one of the world's most dangerous and female-hostile cities, she defies both cultural norms and governmental authorities with her woman-on-a-mission approach.

As I began corresponding with her - learning about the unique challenges she faces on a daily basis - I was compelled to ask one question: What would cause someone like her to not only leave behind family and friends and move to another country, but to risk her life every day in order to walk out her mission? What was her purpose, I asked, for living this kind of life?

As I awaited her answer via email, I thought I knew what was coming. I expected one of those super-spiritual answers - either the bland "I'm here because God asked me to come," or the more inspired, "I'm just trying to walk out the mission of God's Kingdom in the world." I thought she would say that she was just trying to be obedient to God and follow his will for her life. But when I received Christine's email reply, not only did she not give me the expected pat answer, she actually didn't answer my question at all - at least not directly. Instead, she told me a story.

She told of two teen girls - students in her leadership class - who were troubled by the treatment of females in their village. These girls came from a place where women were not only treated as second-class citizens, but as property, trophies, and playthings. Abuse was rampant (though it wasn't seen as vile) and young girls had their dignity, their promise, and sometimes their lives stripped away without anyone offering to give them a voice. Christine was the only one to ever tell these girls that their lives had significance - that they could be something more than a slave or a trophy for a much older man. She must have made a convincing case.

Prompted by their own growing sense of purpose and value, and wanting other women and girls to experience the same, these two young ladies made a decision that could have resulted in their death. They decided to see if they could make a difference in their community by confronting the issue head-on.

With the strange mix of moxie and anxiety that seems to drive people to greatness, they requested a meeting with the tribal elders, and surprisingly, they were granted an audience. In that initial meeting, these two teenagers facilitated a conversation that had never been attempted before, in an effort to change hundreds of years of oppression and abuse of women. They risked their lives for the sake of the future of the other females in their tribe. Their desire for change was so strong that they were willing to risk death for the sake of saving others.

In hearing their story, I was reminded of the biblical story of Esther, the young Jewish girl who used her access to the King to save her people. These two girls, it seems, were made for such a time as this. They stepped into the moment, and like Esther, their objections were heard.

Over the course of several more meetings, the elders had a change of heart. They began to make significant changes to the treatment of women in the tribe. Education became a focus for all the girls in the village. It would take quite a bit of effort to completely overcome the traditional misogynistic culture of the tribe, but changes were afoot - changes that went against thousands of years of tradition - all because of these two girls.

As I read their story, I began to understand purpose in a new way. What was Christine's purpose for living where she did and doing what she was doing? This was it. These stories were what she lived for. When people asked her why she would leave her family and friends behind to go serve in a war zone, this is what she had in mind. Unfortunately, the narrative didn't really fit with what I thought I knew about missions.

DOING IT THE RIGHT WAY

In my mind, I basically divided missions work into two camps - relief work and evangelism. Some missionaries, I recognized, focus on meeting physical needs. Clean water is provided through the digging of wells and distribution of water filters. Orphanages and schools are opened to care for neglected, abandoned, and impoverished children. Mosquito nets, vaccines, and medical clinics care for the physical health of entire communities. The efforts vary across the globe, but the idea is the same - to meet the often dire needs of chronically underserved people.

Some will tell you their primary purpose for these projects is as a pathway to evangelism - that they await the moment someone asks *why* they are doing this. Others will explain that their mission is driven by their desire to care for "the least of these," as commanded in scripture. They long to be the hands and feet of Jesus in the world - a physical representation of God's love for his people. Still others simply feel compelled to do *something*, as a way of giving back to the world - perhaps driven by the recognition of their own privileged upbringing and life.

Whatever the motivation, it's hard to argue against most of these relief-oriented efforts. Support for these types of programs is a no-brainer. Some may contend that it's not really missions work unless you're telling people about Jesus. Others may question the efficiency or effectiveness of a particular program, but the compulsion to help others is certainly understood and applauded, even by those espousing no particular set of religious beliefs. Relief-oriented missions make sense to us.

Then there was the other kind of missionary I had encountered in my life: the evangelist. The goal of the evangelist - their focus and mission in life - is to tell as many people about Jesus as possible, and eventually, to get as many people to follow Jesus as they can (to be saved, to be baptized, to convert, or whatever their terminology).

There are seemingly unlimited ways missionaries go about this kind of work. Some evangelists hold crusades, inviting hundreds, even thousands of people to give their lives to Jesus. Others work one on one, with a focus on personal devotion and discipleship. Evangelists plant churches, lead bible studies, hold crusades, and take any opportunity to share the good news of Jesus with anyone who will listen. They are passionate about their work - just as passionate as the relief workers, but using different methodology with different metrics.

Again, I could appreciate this approach to missions work, even if it wasn't really in my wheelhouse. I understood the command of Jesus to go into all the world and preach the gospel. What a nobel endeavor - one I could admire, if only from afar.

These two categories of missionaries made sense to me. I understood them, and in my limited view, I saw these key drivers as the primary purpose of missions. The purpose for some missionaries was to help others physically. The purpose for others was to help people spiritually. And though both camps seemed to be doing legitimate work, I found myself trying to determine which one was the *right* way to impact the world.

The spiritual, I supposed, was a more long-term effort. After all, the physical stuff will only last maybe 100 years (much less in developing nations with life-expectancy that sometimes doesn't reach 60 years old). So the spiritual stuff was important, but I couldn't shake the fact that Jesus also told us to care for the poor, the orphan, and the widow - to love our neighbor as ourselves. Surely this involved not only spiritual things, but physical as well. I was torn. Which was the correct approach? Which was the *right way*?

Over time, what I discovered is that not only is there no single right way to do missions, but that the missions world is *full* of people and organizations working in ways that fall far outside the boundaries of my two imagined schools of purpose.

REDEFINING PURPOSE

As I began to get more involved in the global missions community, I discovered missionaries of types I never knew existed. Over the past few years, I've met dozens of missionaries involved in local business development - the real, for-profit kind. I've met others who focus on technological innovation, empowering artistic expression, or improving cross-cultural communication. And these perplexing missionaries just keep popping up.

All over the world, from Beijing to Delhi to Caracas, Nairobi to Detroit to Kabul, this new breed of missionaries is investing in the kind of holistic change that not only affects the spiritual climate of their area, but improves the regional economy, raises the aspirations of youth, and challenges the local and global perceptions of previously discounted people.

I thought I knew the purpose of missions, but I found that my definition of purpose was far too narrow. To fully encompass the call of the missionary, we must first recognize the call of all people - a call to die to ourselves and to live and love the way Jesus did.

That kind of love is all-encompassing. It doesn't stop when the water well project is completed. It doesn't end when someone gets baptized. The mission of love that God has sent us all on requires us to invest deeply in people - individually and collectively. It requires us to love and keep loving, to serve and keep serving. It involves the spiritual and the physical, and it's never-ending.

The purpose, then, of missions has almost nothing to do with the tasks being performed, the programs being put in place, or even the souls won for Christ. The purpose of missions is far greater - to embody Jesus, in every possible way, for those we encounter.

In a sense, you could say that the purpose of missions is not really any different than the purpose of Christian life itself. The location and vocation may be different, but the call and the kingdom are the same. We are, truly, in this together.

For a guy who thought he understood missions, this was a revelation. I knew that missions and missionaries were important to those they were serving. I even understood that they were making a significant impact on the church as a whole. What I never knew was just how important they were to people like you and me. I never fully understood that missionaries are beacons for those of us trying to follow Jesus. Their job and their life is an intensely-focused beam of the same kind of light we are all called to be.

This is not to suggest that missionaries are super-saints, or to put pressure on them to be such. It's just that they have answered God's call in a particular way which highlights our own call to be missionaries, wherever we happen to be. That God can use broken and messed up people to impact every tribe and tongue and nation should be of great encouragement to us. It should inspire us to go and love others the way God loves us.

For God so loved the world that he gave everything for us, and for everyone we'll ever encounter, and he asked us to love them like he loved them. What is the purpose of missions? It may sound simple and trite, but the purpose is to love like God loves.

This love is what drives a young woman to move to Uganda to start an orphanage. It's what ignites a retiree to spend his golden years in the favelas of Brazil. This love is the inescapable force that draws people from all walks of life and bids them to drop their proverbial nets and follow in the footsteps of Jesus.

May I be so bold as to suggest that until we begin to understand that kind of love, we will never fully comprehend missions work, nor will we understand the missionaries who have given their lives to sharing God's love with the world.

THE IMPACT OF SHORT-TERM MISSIONS

I WENT ON MY first missions trip when I was in high school. In what has essentially become a right of passage for Christian teens in the U.S., a bus load of us trekked down from our home in the mountains of East Tennessee to a poor border town in the desert of northern Mexico. There, we spent our days helping to demolish dilapidated homes and to build a multi-story orphanage facility. Our nights were filled with the kind of team bonding and spiritual experience that leaves an indelible mark on a young soul.

I returned home with a new perspective on my

American life. It seemed inconceivable that the things I discarded at home - my trash - would literally be seen as treasures by the families I had met in Mexico. While those families lived in makeshift structures in the middle of a city dump, I was quick to toss out anything that didn't meet my exacting standards. I struggled with the materialism that ran rampant in our culture, and I was pleased to have escaped that world, if only for a couple of weeks, to contribute to the betterment of a group of people.

Though that internal struggle dissipated (much more quickly than it should have), and I soon reverted to the typical materialistic life of an American teenager, there was a scar there - a constant reminder that all was not right in the world. That scar remained, invisible to those around me, until the wound was reopened 15 years later in Port au Prince, Haiti.

It had been 8 months since a magnitude 7.0 earthquake had leveled the capital city of this small island nation, killing hundreds of thousands of people, including an entire generation of local university students. The rubble was still everywhere and the makeshift tent cities were quickly becoming permanent residences for the survivors of the quake.

There was a palpable defeatism and hopelessness in the air. As one local told me, "We've worked for 20 years to educate our young people so they could rise up and change this nation. That 20 years is now lost. When they died, our hopes died with them." I came because I felt compelled to do something, but once there, I was unsure what could be done.

While in Haiti, our team helped pour concrete foundations for buildings that still house relief workers to this day. We worshiped at a local church, played with kids from the village, and met with pastors who were trying their best to respond to the devastation all around them. When my time in Haiti was finished, I once again returned home with a sense of accomplishment - happy to have done some good in that place.

You see, that was my understanding of what short-term missions was all about. We spend a few weeks in a place, do a lot of good for the people there, then come home, leaving things at least marginally better off than they were before we came. Behind us, another team will arrive and continue our progress. The whole point, I thought, was to make an impact on the people we were serving. As it turns out, I was vastly overestimating my ability to positively impact the situation.

THE BEST OF INTENTIONS

Building relationships with people on the ground, once again, caused me to reevaluate what I thought I knew about missions. What I've found is that the impact of short-term teams is very different than I imagined. One friend told me of the logistical nightmare of hosting such teams. Others spoke of the relational damage done by well-intentioned, but ill-informed visitors. I even heard stories of projects built by short-term visitors, only to be torn down by locals because the structures either weren't needed or were so poorly built as to not be usable.

You will hear these stories in any area where missions work is prevalent. And after hearing a dozen or more, you may ask yourself, as I did, "What is the point of short-term teams anyway? Do these trips actually have any impact at all?"

In fact, they do. In my gut, I knew they did, but what I never knew is that the greatest impact of short-term missions is not on those *being served*, but rather on those *doing the serving*. I think back on my early short-term experiences, and I realize just how loudly this rings true.

In Mexico, we rose early every morning, largely due to the crowing rooster who planted himself in the tree outside our window. We put on our grubby clothes and heavy duty gloves and worked shoulder to shoulder with a local crew of builders. We dug holes, demolished old structures, mixed concrete, and hung chicken wire to prep for the stucco walls. We worked hard in the hot Mexican sun - a group of teenagers laboring to the point of exhaustion. But in the end, what did we actually accomplish? I'm pretty sure we mostly just got in the way.

We were ostensibly helping to build an orphanage, but the local workers were, by and large, slowed down by our "help." Not only that, but the cost to transport, house, and feed several dozen American teenagers far outweighed the cost of hiring a local, skilled crew to do the work. We weren't actually making a net positive impact on the situation. That's not to say there was no positive impact being made, just that the most significant impact wasn't being made *by* us at all. It was being made *on* us.

Remember, I said I returned from that trip with a scar, and that scar is still with me to this day. God revealed something to me through that trip, and through other trips that followed. *I* was impacted far more than the people I thought I was helping. But you see, that's how short-term missions *really* works.

A MISSIONS LOVE STORY

Sure, there are ways to do short-term better. The stories are numerous of westerners with delusions of riding in on a white horse to rescue the locals (and of locals playing along in order to appease the visitors or to get more assistance). In our ignorance, we've done more harm than good in many parts of the world. So, sure, there are things we can fix, but no matter how good of a program we run, the impact will still typically be felt stronger on the "missionary" than on the local.

And, to some degree, that's OK. In reality, the kind of personal impact made by these short-term trips is a necessary recruiting tool for future long-term missionaries. The scar left on my soul in Mexico is part of the story that brought me to Kenya. And the scars left on so many souls, young and old, continue to inform and persuade people from all over the world to leave behind family and friends in pursuit of God's plan in a far away land.

It's nearly impossible to find a long-term missionary who didn't start out as a short-term missionary. Short-term trips are the missions equivalent of dating (or courting, if you're into that). They help us get to know this intriguing, adventurous "other" known as global missions. They offer a new perspective on the world. They introduce us to people, languages, and entire cultures we may not have otherwise known. And after a few dates, some of us decide to pursue our relationship with missions. Others say, "No thanks!" Some, like me, just let the relationship rest a bit, before picking it up again later.

For those who "click" with their new suitor, the result of those short-term trips is the ignition of a small, but not insignificant flame inside of a would-be missionary. These trips provide a spark for people who will, in time, dedicate their lives to making a considerable mark on the world. The impact is real. It's just different than what I always assumed it to be.

And so, when people ask me what I think about short-term trips, I always reply that I'm cautiously optimistic about them. Short-term teams who recognize the realities of their mission - that they aren't going to have that great of an impact on a culture in two weeks, and that the greater impact will be felt by the people in their group - these teams can experience incredible benefits from short-term trips.

Additionally, short-term teams who are committed to visiting the same place multiple times and building relationships with locals, will see an even greater impact on their own understanding and heart for the people. Through enough visits, they might even find opportunities to make a real difference in the lives of their new-found friends.

CHANGING OUR PITCH

It is through relationship that real change comes about. It's no wonder, then, that quick-hit missions trips to unknown lands often fail to have any real impact on the world's most desperate people and places. The money, time, and manpower that has been invested in short-term missions over the past century is staggering, yet many of those people and places being served have seen very little long-term benefit.

This is why some in the missions community would prefer to do away with short-term trips. They would prefer to spend the money differently, to be more strategic about who is sent and how and when they are sent. And I get it. It's troubling to see a church raise big bucks to send a bunch of teenagers to Mexico, while the local missionaries are struggling to support their ministries financially. But to only look at the downside of these trips is to miss the larger picture.

Fortunately, there are many in the missions community who are advocating for short-term trips. Yes, in many cases, the money could be spent more efficiently, but the fact remains that short-term teams *do* have value, if only churches and missions organizations would change the approach they take to missions.

What would happen if local churches began to view short-term trips differently. What if we took ownership of the fact that the real impact is on *us*? How much more beneficial could short-term trips be if we understood and communicated the developmental and educational nature of these trips to those accompanying us?

What if we got away from the "change the world" language that we use to promote our short-term trips? What if we moved past all the "this is your chance to take the gospel to Haiti" stuff? The gospel is already in Haiti... and Mexico...and Uganda...and Turkey. The good news is already there. *Jesus* is already there and already loving people. What if, instead, we promoted our short-term trips with a little truth-in-advertising. "Experience the world, love people, return changed." That should be the real message of short-term missions.

What if we could begin to develop a kind of missions curriculum in our churches where long-term relationships were built through short-term trips - where impact was measured more by the cultural understanding accrued than by the buildings built or babies held? Maybe then we could begin to see the much sought after fruit of these trips.

After all, fruit is an interesting thing, isn't it? Your satisfaction with the fruit you find is largely dependent upon the fruit you seek. If you look for an apple tree to produce oranges, you will be sorely disappointed. I think it's time we stop looking for the wrong fruit from short-term missions, and begin to seek the fruit that is actually being produced - the changed lives of our participants.

I believe in the value of short-term trips. I've seen the progression from short-term tripper to long-term worker with my own eyes. The contribution of short-term missions to the global missions effort is immense. I simply think we need to understand the real impact of these trips, and adjust our expectations accordingly. If we can do that, then short-term trips can work to benefit the world in even greater ways than we've seen thus far.

THE DEFINITION OF HOME

BORN AND RAISED IN the UK, with a couple of teen years in western Europe, Tina returned to England for university, where she met an adventurous and charming young man named Edward. Edward was from South Africa, where he had grown up during the apartheid era. His desire to escape the segregationist culture of his homeland had led him to pursue academics, and ultimately, to study at a small but prestigious school outside of London. Tina and Edward's mutual friend Teddy had introduced them, and the rest was history.

Two years later, Tina and Edward were married in a small ceremony and they began making plans to move to

Johannesburg. Edward looked forward to beginning his professional career in the land of his father, but Tina had other goals. Having listened for two years to Edward's talk of the changing socio-political climate in South Africa, Tina wondered if there was anything she might be able to offer to those who had been historically oppressed.

Upon arrival in Johannesburg, Edward began his new job, and Tina, having quickly settled into their tiny apartment, started building relationships with some of the locals. She literally stumbled over her mission on their third week in town. The tiny lump of blankets she tripped on while carrying groceries turned out to be Timothy - a child of no more than a week old, who had been abandoned between two cars. Undoubtedly, the mother who left Timothy there was hoping someone like Tina would come along - someone to offer the kind of love and life for this young boy that his biological mom simply couldn't muster.

Thirteen years later, Tina is the director of one of the largest baby rescue centers on the continent of Africa. Her heart has been captured - by the babies, by the city, by her own two boys who have spent their entire lives here.

When Tina's friends speak of the UK as her home, something doesn't ring true. Sure, she enjoys the occasional treats that remind her of her childhood, but each year when she visits her old hometown, it feels less and less like her true home.

Many of her old friends have moved away. Others have changed drastically. But perhaps the hardest relationships to maintain are the people who seem not to have changed at all, and expect Tina to be the same as well. They scoff at her acquired accent, laugh when she uses an Afrikaans phrase that sounds like gibberish to them, and wonder aloud if it isn't about time she moves "back home."

For Tina, there is no home. Even though she has adapted to life in South Africa, a single conversation with her makes it obvious to any local that she isn't one of them. To make matters worse, her husband's success in business causes some local women to resent her. After all, she, a Brit, stole one of "their" men.

Tina finds herself in a city where her husband is native, she is anything but, and her kids are stuck somewhere in the middle. She can't imagine dragging them back to England, but there are days when she wonders how long she can stay in Jo'burg. The rescue center pretty much runs itself now, and she *does* long for home. If only she could figure out where home is.

For Tina, like so many missionaries, the longing for home is quickly thwarted by the fact that home no longer exists. Tina imagines starting a completely new life, in a completely new home - one of her choosing. Tahiti perhaps. Then she realizes that even a tropical island can't replace the friends, family, geography, and culture which has somehow slipped through her fingers. Not only that, but for her husband and sons, any place outside of Jo'burg is a foreign land.

So she stays. She longs for what she can't have. She struggles to understand what she does have. Meanwhile, well-meaning friends say ignorant things about why she won't just come home.

WHERE THE HEARTS ARE

It's been said that home is where the heart is - a saying which, itself, hints at the inherent struggle of missionaries when they think of "home." For the brand new missionary, the significance (and definition) of home is undeniable. Home is where you came from, where you grew up, where most of your life experience happened. It's the place you'll go back to on vacation, holiday, or furlough.

For many missionaries, however, the significance of that place tends to fade over time. Indeed, the very definition of home begins to make a transformation. Home becomes two places and no place at all. The "where the heart is" concept only confuses the matter, as the heart of a missionary points at once toward their family home (their old friends, relatives, places, and culture) *and* toward their current missions home (new friends, adopted family, places, and culture).

Even the healthiest of missionaries will tell you there are days when, if their heart wasn't in it, they would hop on a plane and leave. It is absolutely necessary to engage your mission at the heart level if you're to have any hope of lasting long-term. So, if home is where the heart is, it's understandable that many missionaries don't quite know where to call home.

To make matters worse, the home you left a year ago - or 5 or 10 - no longer exists. People change, families move away, and life goes on. This is especially true if your friends were young when you left. Life transitions happen often during the early years of adulthood, and the lives of all those old friends can change drastically in the course of just a few years. That 20-something, single friend, who used to drop everything when you came for a visit, is now in her early thirties with a full-time job, a husband, 3 kids, and a hyper-active social calendar. She's still happy you're home, and will go to great lengths to make time for you, but it just isn't the same.

Sometimes, as a returning missionary, *same* is what you want. You crave *same-ness*. You want familiarity when you return to your former home. You want a life you can settle into like a comfortable old arm chair. What you discover, though, is that someone has replaced that old chair with a fancy new one. It might not be a bad chair. It might be better than the old one. But it's not the *same*. As one missionary friend put it, "I don't feel at home anywhere. Wherever I am, I long for the other place."

Please understand, these struggles aren't exclusive to missionaries. Anyone who has moved away from their "home" and later returned can attest to the fact that you can't simply press the pause button on those relationships, only to pick up where you left off later. For missionaries, however, this is complicated by the fact that everyone *expects* you to just *love* being "home."

"Aren't you so glad to be back," they'll say. "I bet you've missed it here." Most people who have never lived abroad can't begin to imagine that you actually *enjoy* your life, especially if you live in a less-developed locale. They understand, at least in part, the concept of missionary *calling*, but few can comprehend that you might actually *prefer* living where you do to living "back home."

AN IMPOSSIBLE CHOICE

In my conversations with missionaries, most are quick to point out the unique joys of doing what they're doing and living where they're living. I've lost count of the number of people who say, "I'm so thankful I got to raise my kids here," or, "My relationship with my spouse is so much better since we moved here." Sure, not everyone has a positive experience in their host country, but many do. For those missionaries, the idea of moving "home" is terrifying. In fact, many who have lived abroad for years struggle mightily to adapt upon returning to their native country.

As one missionary friend recently told me, "If only I could combine my two 'homes,' I would gladly take the bad with the good." In other words, missionaries aren't idealistic dreamers who want the best of both worlds. They are realists who understand the limitations of both worlds, but who have a strong connection to both. They live in a kind of residential purgatory - stuck between their old life and their new, their former home and their current one. Those of us who think of ourselves as supporters and encouragers of missionaries desperately need to understand this dynamic.

But how can we understand it if we've never lived it? How can Tina's friend in Glasgow even begin to relate to her situation? I've found the following metaphor to be useful.

Imagine that you are a young parent. You have one child - a 5 year old - who means the world to you. This is your only child, and the only child you've ever loved. You would do anything for this child. Then, a few years later, another child comes along. Now, you have two. Your love for the first hasn't diminished one bit, but you also have an incredible connection with the second.

The older both kids get, the more they compete for your time, attention, and affection. You love them both dearly, but neither seems satisfied with you - both of them constantly demanding more. It's a frustrating existence - torn between these two loves - but you embrace it. It is, after all, your only choice.

Now imagine that someone comes along and tries to fix your problem. "Just leave one kid behind," they tell you. "Both of them are getting older now. I'm sure if you left the youngest with a loving family, you could go on to have a great life with the eldest - your firstborn, the first child you ever loved."

Silly isn't it? To ask a parent to choose between two kids is not a form of love or encouragement. It is, instead, the kind of choice reserved for victims of abuse and terror. Meanwhile, every day, some missionary somewhere is being told that the solution to his or her problem is to make the same kind of choice about "home."

A word to the wise for anyone who is trying to love missionaries well: If you're question begins with, "Why can't you just…," you probably need to rethink it. As we have already discovered, and will continue to observe throughout this book, missionary life is never as simple as it appears. Everything is complex.

Trips "home" are emotional roller coasters, swirling from elation to despair to anticipation to fear. The same occurs on the return trip, as the familiarity of the host country brings a sense of relief, but the people, places, and life left behind seem to call out from beyond the aircraft doors.

Let's face it. There is no way to fix this. Sure, we can offer pithy answers like, "Your home is in heaven, not on earth," or "Home is wherever your family is," but we don't get it. We don't get it because it isn't our life. It isn't our family. It isn't our home. Like a ship torn from its moorings, missionaries are adrift at sea between their two homes. To fully embrace one is to lose the other - a choice few would choose to make.

Our job, then, is not to fix it. It's not even to fully understand it. Our job is to listen, to empathize, and to the best of our ability, to lessen the blow. Rather than asking a parent to choose between two children, our role is to encourage the missionary in the journey. Rather than saying "Why can't you just…," we should be saying,

"What can I do to help?"

There are certain parts of missionary life that are permanent. Loss of a true home is one. Whether you're away for 2 years or 30, once you become a missionary, you are never a native again. Once the second child comes along, you will never again be the parent of only one. May we strive to help our missionary friends embrace this reality and to live well in their odd and exciting multi-home-and-no-home world.

THE ROLE OF THE SENDER

WE ALL KNOW THAT the hands-on work of missions is done by the missionary - the person in the field, face to face with the people, the culture, and the issues to be addressed. But what is our role - those of us who send out missionaries from our churches? What part do we play in this missions business, and is it as simple as some have made it out to be? In our efforts to go into all the world, how can we send well?

Attempting to describe the various players in missions, there's a phrase commonly used in the missions community: Pray, Give, Go. Missions work, it is said, relies on people who are willing to do these three things.

Not everyone can go do the work. Not everyone has resources to give. Everyone *can* pray, but let's be realistic, not everyone *will*. So, the theory goes, some will pray for the work, some will finance the work, and some will do the work.

This pray, give, go model actually provides an excellent snapshot of our involvement in missions. I've used it myself. It's easy to remember, it hits on the high points, and if we're honest, it gives reluctant people an easy way out. "I don't have any desire to go, but I'll give," or "I don't have any money to give, but I'll pray."

There's nothing wrong with this little phrase, but I've discovered it is woefully inadequate to describe the unending assortment of roles involved in successful missions work. There is no mention of coaching and mentorship, no focus on logistical, pastoral, or emotional support. There's not a hint of cultural training and awareness, or of soliciting input and listening to local voices.

Sure, you might be able to squeeze some of those into the "give" or "go" roles, but few people would naturally do so. No, most people think like I once thought. The role of the missionary is to do the work. The role of the sending church, organization, friends, and family is to pray and send money.

This is actually a pretty good deal for the senders. In this mode of thinking, I get the enjoyment of fulfilling the Great Commission simply by tossing a prayer up to God on occasion (as long as the missionary sends me some "prayer points") and by setting up a monthly auto-draft from my bank account. In so doing, I am actually shouldering two thirds of the "Pray, Give, Go" burden. I'm praying. I'm giving. Someone else can do the going.

The problem, of course, is that praying and giving are the easy parts. They are also the parts often left undone when life gets hectic. Meanwhile, the missionary in the field - the one responsible for the "go" - has to press on, regardless of the efforts of others, or lack thereof.

I recently had a chat with Carl, a missionary friend who was struggling to keep his ministry afloat. His orphanage houses several hundred kids and employs a couple dozen local workers. His social media profiles have thousands of followers, friends, likes, and all the rest. The bank account, however, tells a different story.

Sure, he can raise money for new projects. Need a new van? Done. A new building? Done. But what about the monthly funding to feed, clothe, and educate the children? What about the ongoing support needed to pay for fuel, electricity, and staffing costs? It has all but dried up.

Carl, a long-term missionary for over 15 years now, sums it up by saying, "I know people have other things to spend their money on, but while it's easy for them to not send their check this month, it's not as easy for me to tell the kids they can't eat."

As senders, we too often miss this reality. For us, when we cut our missions budget, it shows up as a line item in a spreadsheet. For Carl, it shows up as 20 bags of rice, or a truck load of clean water, or a month's worth of cooking fuel that he no longer has the resources for. Carl needs the prayers. He needs the giving. But even when they don't come, he still has to do the going.

Of course, the struggles between missionaries and senders run much deeper than lack of funding or prayer commitment. These things are easily understood, if not easily remedied. I knew that, as senders, we sometimes fail in these areas. What I never knew is that we also fail our missionaries by minimizing our role in their lives.

THE TOOLBOX IS EMPTY

I used to think the role of sender was limited to praying and giving. What I've come to understand is that if we limit our role to these traditional areas of support, we leave our missionary friends without some basic institutional and individual needs. Even if we give them an abundance of prayer and financial support, refusal to fully embrace the other facets of our role will shorten the lifespan of these ministries, and sometimes of the missionaries themselves.

My friend Jim is a psychologist with extensive cross-cultural experience and training. Part of his job is to work with missionaries who have reached the end of their rope. He leads debrief sessions for missionaries returning home. He takes teams around the world to offer spiritual direction and times of refreshing for struggling missionaries. He even coaches church leaders on how to be good senders.

In reflecting on what he has learned from working with hundreds of missionaries and their sending churches, Jim challenges the senders, saying, "One of the greatest travesties of missions work is that we proudly send missionaries into all the world, but fail to equip them with even the basic tools needed to do the work"

Too often, we place the full weight of the Great Commission on the person being sent, and then we sit in a board meeting and decide whether or not the job they're doing warrants our support. We separate the calling of the missionary from the calling of the sender. If they fail, it's on them, not us. We did our part.

Except we haven't done our part. In fact, in my experience talking with and working directly with missionaries, I can only think of maybe four cases where the senders were actually holding up their end of the bargain. Four.

From large international organizations to small local churches, we are failing our missionaries. We are neglecting our calling. We simply aren't sending well.

Here are a few questions to consider when determining if you are sending well:

1. When was the last time you spoke directly with the

missionary or missionaries you support?

2. When was the last time you had an in-depth conversation about the realities of their life (not just talking about their ministry)?

3. Can you name 3 significant challenges they face on a daily basis?

4. Do you know their biggest logistical concern?

5. What steps have you taken to ensure they have strong pastoral support from a local pastor in their country, as well as from your church?

6. What plans do you have to support them spiritually, emotionally, and physically when they return to your country, whether short-term or long-term?

7. What do the people of your church know about the missionaries you support? Do you talk about them regularly, or are they merely poster children for a special Sunday where you brag about your work in the world?

8. *When did you last visit them, and how much time did you spend one-on-one?*

Did you have quick answers to those questions? Did some of them make you uncomfortable? Did you realize that you are a bit aloof when it comes to your missions partners?

Knowing *about* the work of a missionary is much different from *knowing* them. As senders, we can't just be concerned with the missions *widget* - the bottom line product of missionary work. We must be concerned with the individual. We must be concerned with the process. We must be concerned with the toll it takes on those involved. In short, we need to act more like a parent and less like a CEO in our missions efforts.

Missionaries are not "human capital," they are people, created in God's image and called by him to get their hands dirty doing the work that he has *also* called you to participate in. As senders, we don't get the luxury of cutting a check and walking away. To truly give to missions is about more than money. It is an investment of time, resources, and personal energy that never subsides as long as the work of the mission is ongoing.

Sending out a missionary is like birthing a child. You can never relinquish that responsibility. Sure, they might eventually find their own financial provision. They might grow into a mature organization. But you are still the parent. You are still the sender, and as such, you have a responsibility to pastor, to equip, to lead, to encourage, to understand, to empathize, to invite others along, to cheerlead, to challenge, to pray, to give, and yes, to go.

CONSTANT CONTACT

I was watching a nature program the other day where a group of conservationists were working to grow the population of endangered species. Their methodology was similar to what I've seen and read about before. They first took injured or abandoned animals, typically young ones, and nursed them to health. Then, these babies, which would have otherwise died, were slowly acclimated to a more typical natural habitat. After that, they were released into the wild.

But there is an important step that happens just before

their release that I think applies well to our work of sending missionaries. You see, before this animal is released back into the wild, he is tagged with a microchip. Undetectable to the eye (or any other senses) of the surrounding animals, this chip serves as a way of checking up on the animal.

Movement can be tracked, vital signs monitored, even interaction within the herd can be observed. If there is a problem, this team of scientists has their finger on the pulse of it. If the animal is rejected by the others, they know about it. If there is some kind of systemic issue, they will be the first on the scene. Why? Because they invested the time, energy, and resources to make sure they could be in intimate contact with that animal no matter what.

While I would caution against implanting microchips in your missionaries, I think you get the point. As senders, we can't simply say a prayer, write a check, and put the missionary on a plane. We must invest the time, energy, and resources to develop systems and responses which adequately support our missions partners. Anything less is neglect.

To call ourselves partners or supporters, we have to have our finger on the pulse of the missionaries we support. Otherwise, we're simply donors. Or worse, casual observers. If we are doing our job, then our missionary friends should see us as a truly valuable asset to their ministry, beyond any money we raise. Likewise, we should see our missionary partners as a vital piece of our own ministry - walking out that portion of our calling that we are unable to physically walk out on our own.

What I never knew about the role of the sender is that it is, first and foremost, a relational role. The responsibility of the sender is to care more than everyone else. If we will seek first to love and care for the missionary, then we will be able to fulfill our responsibility to the mission.

The Apostle Paul warns us in 1 Corinthians 13 that there is a whole world of good we can do - gifts we can utilize, goals we can obtain, faith we can possess - but if we do not love, we fail. We are nothing.

Let that be a challenge to us as senders. How well do we love our missionary friends? Do we have our finger firmly on the pulse of their life, their family, their passions, and their pain? Or are we just gongs and clanging cymbals - making lots of noise about our work in the world, while neglecting the workers we sent out?

WHAT I KNEW I DIDN'T KNOW

I KNOW NOTHING ABOUT quantum physics. I know the field of study exists, and I think it has something to do with particles and quarks and the makeup of the universe, but that's the extent of my knowledge, and that probably isn't even right. (Apologies to any quantum physicists who read that last sentence.) I truly and honestly know nothing about the subject.

The thing is, I *know* I don't know anything about quantum physics. I would never pretend to know anything about the field. I certainly wouldn't write a blog post or an article or even an online comment related to quantum physics. It's completely outside my realm of knowledge. I'm fully aware of that.

This awareness, I think, is of vital importance, not only in quantum physics, but also in the church. I've known too many people in my life who, through a complete lack of self-awareness, were convinced they knew about something when they really didn't. Some of them are also really good at convincing other people that they know what they're talking about. I've even been one of those hopelessly unaware people (see the previous chapters).

However, in my endeavor to comprehend the missions world, even though I had innumerable assumptions and misunderstandings, there was also a fair amount of knowledge I knew I didn't possess - things I *knew* I didn't know. Some things, I realized, simply can't be known until you are living in the situation. Others, I supposed, can never really be known or understood at all.

What I do know how to do is ask questions!

I'm the father of two young girls. Our oldest is five years old at the time of this writing, and her favorite word is *why*. Her *why* never ends. In the last 24 hours, I've been asked why we need bushes, why God is everywhere, why we hiccup, why we need to be happy, why we have legs, and why there are states. My little girl is an inquisitive soul. When she doesn't know the answer, she asks a question.

Nothing is off-limits to her (as evidenced by the many questions I would rather not share here). There is no pride or ego to get in the way of her questions. At five years old, she doesn't even know which things she's *supposed* to know and which ones she isn't, so there's no self-conscious voice inside saying, "You should already know that," or, "You're not supposed to know that yet."

As a father, of course, all these questions can be taxing. I love having conversations with my little peanut, but sometimes, I have to put a moratorium on the questions, especially when they start to move into the realm of silliness.

I must admit there are times when I'm afraid my missionary friends look at me and see a five year old inquisitor. Though I try not to pepper them with questions, sometimes the questions roll out...and keep rolling. And the reason is simple. Just like my five year old little girl, I really want to know. I want to understand. I can't live other people's lives, so I'm trying my best to get a good picture of what their lives are like. As far as I'm concerned, that's the only way I can be a good friend and pastor to them. If I don't know something, I have to ask questions.

QUESTION YOUR QUESTIONS

In an effort to learn what I could, I set out to understand what life is really like for a missionary. I asked questions of myself, based on my own observations. I harassed my missionary friends in an attempt to find the answers to my questions. I compiled information, then returned to my friends to ask if what I was perceiving was, indeed, reality.

There is a difference, however, between asking questions which seek to understand, and asking questions which are just passive-aggressive accusations. "Do you really think you're making any difference over there?" is not going to elicit a very positive response. It might be a *strong* response, but nobody is going to leave that conversation feeling warm and fuzzy all over. So, when I'm asking questions of my missionary friends, I focus on really trying to understand their life, without attempting to judge it.

A question like, "Tell me about the biggest challenges you are currently facing," is actually an invitation for the other individual to choose the topic - to set the agenda. Maybe their biggest challenge in that moment has to do with their kids. Maybe it's a conflict with a co-worker.

Maybe it's the price of diesel fuel.

The way we ask questions is important, and it's something I am constantly seeking to get better at. I would encourage you to do the same. As I speak with missionaries, one of the common refrains I hear is that other people "just don't get it." Sometimes, they don't get it because the missionary is a poor communicator. Missionaries have to own that piece of things. But sometimes, when people don't get it, it's because they (we) have leaned too heavily on pre-conceived notions and assumptions, rather than taking the time to simply ask good questions, dig deeper, and really get below the surface.

One missionary friend recently responded to a series of accusatory questions (from someone else, not from me) by simply saying, "I would love for you to come here so I can show you what I'm talking about." Truth is, until you've experienced the life of a missionary, whether urban or rural, in a developed nation or an undeveloped one - until you have lived their reality, even if for a short time, you can't hope to even remotely understand what their life is like.

This is why I am so adamant about visiting the missionaries we support. Find the money and go. It's that important. In fact, the first trip I took to Kenya - the one that set the course for our move here - was funded out of my own pocket. It was a last-minute trip that was far outside our meager church budget, but I knew it was important, so I picked up the tab.

It was on that trip that I began, I believe, to ask good questions. And the responses to those questions sent me down a path that would ultimately lead me right back to where I am today - over 8,000 miles from our family and our native culture, and loving every minute of it. (OK, *almost* every minute of it.)

A JOURNEY OF DISCOVERY

You see, I had a lot of questions, but as I began to collect responses, I realized that the majority of my questions could really be boiled down to just a handful of main inquiries. They involved questions of every day life: What does an ordinary day look like for a missionary (if there even is such a thing)? They touched on some of the ministry challenges present for missionaries: What are the costs, both personally and organizationally, of doing missions work? Some were pastoral in nature: What kind of support do missionaries really need most? Some had to do with personal relationships and interaction with others: What is it like to truly embrace a new culture and the people within it?

These are the categories of questions that kept me awake at night as I began to dive deeper and uncover a missionary world much different than the one I had previously imagined. The things I knew I didn't know are the things I sought to understand. The things I discovered, I now share with you. This is certainly not a comprehensive list of everything I've learned or everything I'm still attempting to learn, but it's a start. Perhaps one day I'll be forced to write another volume of things I didn't know!

These are my learnings, gleaned from many conversations over the past several years. I continue to add to them daily. I continue to refine them. More than anything, I continue to try to put into practice the wisdom that my missionary friends are gracious enough to share with me. I hope you will do the same.

Perhaps something written here will open your eyes to

the many parts of missionary life you want to understand better. Maybe it will cause you to ask good questions of your missionary friends. Maybe it will be the beginning of some open, honest conversations. If so, then every word written here, every question and every answer, has been worth the time and energy invested. May you become a better caretaker of these relationships through the many conversations which are driven by a desire to understand the things you know you don't know.

THE EVERY DAY LIFE OF A MISSIONARY

IT WAS ALWAYS HARD for me to imagine what missionary life was like. I understood there was hardship - that the adventure piece was probably regularly overtaken by other realities. Some missionaries, I understood, live in very primitive conditions, some in hotbeds of violence. It seems like every missionary you meet has had a run in with a poisonous creature, a corrupt government official, or a mysterious disease.

Although I knew these were the highlights (nay, lowlights) of missionary life, I could never, no matter how hard I tried, conceive of what a *normal* day looked like for these people. Though I was pretty sure they started and ended their day with an hour of prayer and meditation, the stuff that went on in the middle was a mystery, like the contents of a hot dog. I could see the sausage, but I couldn't understand how it was made.

A gross analogy perhaps, but I think it's pretty applicable to missionary life and the way we outsiders interact with it. The fact is, we don't *want* to know how the sausage was made. We like to look at pretty pictures of finished projects - water shooting out of a tap, or people worshiping in a newly-constructed church building. But the stuff that happens day in and day out is best left behind the veil.

Of course, this means we have no real idea what our missionary friends are going through on a daily basis. It also means that we sometimes fill in the gaps. We turn the lives of our friends into some kind of fairy tale - one where the good guy always wins, the bad guy always wears a black hat, and every day is filled with swashbuckling adventure.

But as it turns out, everyday missionary life can actually be quite unremarkable. Before the advent of modern technology and medical advancements, missionaries spent much of their time writing letters, struggling to communicate with locals, and battling their own contraction of indigenous diseases. Today's missionaries have more technological and medical tools at their disposal, but most live a life filled with blog updates, email newsletters, car repair, and long lines to pay the power bill. Many missionaries spend more time behind a desk than they do out in the field, and much more time on their feet than on their knees.

This is the life of a missionary - not that different from the life you might live. Some of the difficulties are unique to a particular locale, others are universal, but if you listened in on the prayers of most missionaries, you would find that many of their primary concerns mirror your own - marriages and kids, personal health and the health of others, financial struggles and relational conflict.

Missionary life is tough, but in some ways, it's not so different from your life and mine. Everyone has hardship. Everyone has pain. Though missionary life may bring a different set of difficulties, the anxiety is the same, as is the necessary response.

A BALANCING ACT

But what about the exotic stuff? The life of a missionary can't be all spread sheets and boiling water. After all, these are people living in strange lands, surrounded by unique cultures and languages. Aren't their lives at least somewhat more exciting and adventurous than yours? In a word, *yes*.

Of course missionaries live crazy and exciting lives! Those stories they tell while on furlough aren't fabrications, they just don't give the complete picture. Encounters with giant arachnids or guerrilla militias or angry baboons may not be every day occurrences, but they do happen, and they make for great stories later. (Have you ever noticed that all the best missionary stories contain at least one "I could have died" moment. We are a morbid people.)

Having spent time with missionaries, talking about their everyday lives, I've come to understand a little about this strange dichotomy. One day, you're rescuing a child out of a ditch, the next, you're lecturing your own kid about cleaning his room, and the next, you're negotiating the price of mangos at the market.

All of these moments - the fascinating and the familiar, the somber and the sublime - merge together into one life. That's what I never knew about the life of a missionary - that this life requires the ability to balance such extremes.

So, for the sake of education, let me give you a glimpse into the life of an ordinary missionary.

AN AVERAGE DAY

Luke is a normal guy. He was an average student in school, went to a middle-of-the-road college, got a boring degree, and resigned himself to an 8-5 job to pay the bills. Then, something happened to Luke. He got sucked into the missionary life.

It started out as short trips to Nigeria, which led to a month in Uganda, and finally a year of service in Kenya. Then he took the plunge. Luke has now lived in Kenya for 5 years. His life here, like most missionaries, is one of extremes.

Luke lives on $2000 per month, which is about half the salary he was making in the U.S., but with the lower cost of living, he's able to pay the bills, eat, and have a little left over each month. He lives in a rented house - one much larger and on a better lot than anything he could afford in the U.S. He has a full-time housekeeper, about whom he never writes on his blog or social media sites, for fear of judgmental comments. ("Boy, that must be nice to have someone to wash your dishes!")

You see, "house help" is part of the economy here. A westerner like Luke is expected to employ at least one or two people (who, in turn, will employ house help of their own). He pays his housekeeper about $85 per month, which is the going rate. For this, he gets a clean house, complete with the daily sweeping and mopping required in a dusty, open-air, non-air conditioned environment. He doesn't have a dishwasher, clothes washer, or dryer, so his housekeeper hand washes and line dries everything.

When Luke first got to Kenya, he hired a housekeeper and decided to be generous and pay her double the going rate. She quit after 3 months, having accrued the equivalent of 6 months worth of pay. He has since learned that it is actually more beneficial to all parties to pay the standard local rate than to pay something the locals consider exorbitant - to work within the local economy rather than bucking against it. The second housekeeper he hired, whom he pays a more normal wage, has been with him for over 4 years, and has referred several friends for jobs with Luke's network of contacts.

With his housekeeper caring for the house, Luke has more time to work with the local street kids - his primary mission. He spends his days interacting with the five boys he is helping to send to school, as well as with their group of friends, who have decided that school is for losers. He is a father figure to these boys - with all the support, encouragement, discipline, and love he can muster - which is a difficult task having never had kids, and without the advantages of having raised them from infancy.

It's not an easy job. Most days, there is some sort of conflict between the boys, or between Luke and one of the boys, or both. There are typical teen problems like girls, booze, and school. Then there are the unique situations faced by abandoned, neglected boys who have had to fend for themselves for most of their lives - in some cases, a decade or more. They are mature beyond their years in many of the most dreadful ways, and woefully immature in other vital aspects of life.

Luke's days are filled with hard work and relational investment. At the end of the day, he returns home exhausted, glad to have a brief respite from the insanity, if only for the night.

Most nights, during and after dinner, he has a couple of glasses of wine (even though his sending missions board wouldn't approve), catches up on emails, and watches an American movie or TV show. He made the decision to splurge on satellite TV after living here 6 months. It's fairly pricey, but it's also the only entertainment option available. There are no cinemas, no malls, no concert venues, and generally, no fun things to do. So, TV has become the go-to downtime activity.

After watching a little TV and finishing his second glass of wine, Luke usually likes to sit back and read. Sometimes he reads his bible, other times a leadership book, and occasionally a novel. He finds that his reading habits mirror his life - a combination of spiritual, pragmatic, and frivolous.

His spiritual life ebbs and flows. Sometimes he prays and reads his bible regularly, and other times those things slide to the back burner. He is serious about God, but finds it hard to make a habit of those tried and true spiritual disciplines people always talk about. He has a lot of guilt about this, and doesn't ever talk about his struggle. He knows a lot of people would be disappointed to learn of this missionary's lack of discipline.

Luke's social life is almost nonexistent. He has a few friends, but they are as busy as he is, and they only gather on special occasions. Almost any time someone says, "Hey Luke, do you know so-and-so," the answer is no. To be honest, Luke stopped trying to make friends a long time ago. People come and go, daily life is exhausting, and his waking hours are filled with ministry work. Security can be a concern in the evening, so everyone typically stays home after dark. It can get pretty lonely.

It's not that his life is bad, it's just complicated. It's hard for him to explain to others how missionary life is so rewarding, but sometimes depressing. It's adventurous, but sometimes boring. It's immersive, but sometimes solitary. There are aspects of his old home in the U.S. that he really misses, and others he's glad to be rid of. The things he longs for - friends, a church community, a good Thai restaurant - are often on his mind, but at the same time, his new existence is rich with the things his old life never had.

Through his ministry work, he knows he is making a difference in the lives of a group of boys, which motivates him to get out of bed each morning. His embrace of local culture has introduced him to new perspectives, new foods, and an enhanced faith in God. Most of the time - 8 days out of 10 - he can't imagine living anywhere else. He loves his life in Kenya. The other 2 days, he's ready to pack up and go back to the U.S.

He knows his old friends in the U.S. would never understand, so he doesn't talk to them about his life. He just shares ministry updates, pictures of food, and comments about his latest TV show obsession. It's easier that way.

DIGGING DEEPER

Unfortunately, that's why people like you and me are unable to get a good picture of the everyday life of a missionary. When you ask your missionary friend about their life, what they share will likely only scratch the surface. There's so much more they wish they could tell you, but they're sure you don't want to hear it and couldn't understand it even if they told you.

But if you care for your friend, take the time to dig a little deeper. Suspend judgement of their lives, and instead, offer a huge helping of grace, and attempt to understand both their joys and their struggles. Admit when you don't get it, but validate their experience. Become a trusted and empathetic ear for your missionary friends and you will gain valuable insight into what real life is like on the mission field.

I knew I didn't fully understand the life of a missionary. What I never knew is how much their life is like yours and mine. Maybe the highs are higher, but the lows might be lower. In the end, they need friends who will journey together with them, even if some of those friends are thousands of miles away. Let's be people committed to being involved in the every day lives of our missionary friends.

THE COST OF DOING MISSIONS

YOU KNOW THOSE TELEVISION investigative reports and online exposés about big charities? The ones where they tell you where your money is really going - how the top executive earns a six-figure salary and a good portion of your donation goes to soliciting more donations, or to so-called administrative costs?

Were you shocked to learn about a fleet of vehicles purchased with donated funds, or of the vast real estate holdings of a multi-national non-profit organization? Have you ever stopped giving to a charity based on one of those reports? I hope not. I hope you cared enough to do a little more research.

You see, the trouble with these tell-all reports is that they rarely tell all. That is, they tend to lean in a direction that is wholly sensational, not wholly truthful, and certainly not the whole story. Sure, there are non-profit organizations which are poorly managed, where money flows like water into ill-conceived and poorly executed ideas.

There are even some charities that are downright scams, where piles of cash flow to a handful of people, none of whom are the groups supposedly being helped. But for every legitimate report about an organization out of control, there are a dozen ill-researched (or worse, intentionally skewed) stories designed to disparage groups of people who are truly working for good.

The major players get named and slammed. The public face of the organization is maligned. The board of directors gets nervous. Press releases are issued, policies changed, and executives ousted. But among smaller missions agencies, NGOs, and relief organizations, many cringe as they see these reports, because they know their books look very similar…or worse.

The leaders of these small organizations fly way under the radar of local, national, and international media, but they know that if they came under the same scrutiny as the big guys, they could be in trouble. And in many cases, if just a few donors pulled out, their operation could be shut down for good. They also know that, media or no media, as they wrestle daily with the financial realities of their good work, others are looking on with a critical eye, leery of where their donations are going.

LEARNING FROM LOUISE

Here's the difficult truth: doing good costs a lot of money, takes an enormous amount of time (which, when paying employees, means even more money), and requires highly skilled and motivated people - people who are often pulled from the business world, where six-figure salaries are on the low end of the pay scale. Operations large and small are constantly faced with the fact that they are required to spend a significant portion of their income on these administrative expenses. Nobody likes it. It's not the way anyone would prefer things to work. It's just the reality of the situation.

So let's forget about those big guys for a moment. Let's

look at a typical small-scale international relief operation.

Louise is a sower of seeds…literally. In an average year, she distributes seeds to around 500 farmers in West Africa. Louise doesn't take a salary, but does have a small budget of $1000 per month to cover her housing and food expenses. She also has workers who help interview farmers, pack seeds, and transport the product from her small warehouse to the villages where she works, at a cost of $21,000 annually.

The warehouse itself has two workers - a manager and a security guard - along with two very old, very temperamental pickup trucks. Between the warehouse rental, the two employees, and the fuel and maintenance on the two clunkers, Louise spends about $35,000 annually.

Then there are the government fees - some legitimate, and some not so much - which she is forced to pay in order to operate in this region. Last year, she paid over $3000 to local and national government agencies.

All this - $71,000 in total - is in addition to the cost of seed, which is around $15,000 per year, and the cost to ship the seed to the warehouse, which is another $4000.

Louise's total annual budget is $90,000, or about $180 for each farmer she helps. She knows that for every $180 investment, the yield will not be only one crop, but years worth of crops for her recipients, and that the investment of $180 is well-spent to feed a family for a decade or more.

However, Louise can also do the math. If put under a microscope, she knows her allocation of funds could be called into question. By some overly-aggressive calculation methods, she spends nearly 80% of the money given to her organization on administrative costs. Even when using more generous calculations, Louise admits that well over 40% of her organization's income goes to staff and facilities expenses.

A large organization with those same percentages would be on the receiving end of a public outcry, but Louise has trimmed costs as much as she can. Helping people is expensive, and there's little she can do about it. She tries to reassure herself by pointing out that not only is she helping those 500 farmers each year, but she's also helping her small staff, the owner of her rented house, the warehouse landlord, and the company where she buys the seed. But would anyone else see the value in this? It keeps her awake at night.

The reality Louise is facing is what is known in the business world as *CODB - cost of doing business.* In the for-profit world, CODB is accepted as a necessary evil. If you want to run a successful laundromat or gas station, there is certain overhead - real estate expenses, specialized equipment, etc. - for which you have to pay. If you open a pharmacy or medical clinic, you need highly educated, specialized personnel, like pharmacists or medical professionals, which come at a price.

The business world knows this, and they gladly pay what it takes to operate a profitable, efficient business. Even their shareholders - a notoriously frugal bunch - understand these business realities. In the non-profit and missionary world, however, some seem to expect those costs to simply disappear.

Surely people who are doing good in the world won't have high administrative costs. Why would an organization have to *spend* money on fundraising? Why should an executive get paid such a large salary? How can it take so any people to do this work? Louise knows why.

In her organization, she makes all the phone calls, sends all the emails, and updates the website, but if her operation was larger, she would need to pay people to handle each of those things. She has an accountant friend in North Carolina who does the books for free, but she knows if she continues to grow, that job will become too time-consuming for her friend to handle on the side. Besides, she already feels bad for not being able to pay for those services.

Louise has a young doctor friend back in the U.S. who loves coming to visit her each year. She hosts clinics about hygiene and nutrition, helping to educate the farmers and their families on ways to stay healthy. Her friend would one day like to come and work with Louise full time. She would do it now if not for the student loans she faces after being in medical school for the better part of a decade.

Others may not understand why staff costs are so high in non-profits, but they also don't stop to consider that even someone with a good heart has to pay the bills and put food on the table. A doctor of the caliber of Louise's friend could earn nearly a half million dollars a year back home, but if a non-profit were to pay a quarter of that, many people would think it excessive. Louise imagines being able to hire her young friend and pay her even enough to cover the repayment of her school loans - the monthly equivalent of a home mortgage. What a huge difference they could make together.

When things are going well, Louise envisions ramping up her operation to help more people. What would it take to help 1,500 farmers each year - or 5,000? At some point, Louise's meager business skills would be tapped out, and she would be forced to hire someone who knew how to run a sizable non-profit organization. She might be able to find an incredibly talented, and equally charitable, individual, but even at a deeply discounted salary, someone like that - a CEO who actually knew what he or she was doing - would cost a sizable chunk of change. In short, Louise knows she may one day be able to make her percentages look better, but she'll never be able to avoid the *CODM - the cost of doing missions*.

THE PRICE OF TRUST

Until recently, I hadn't considered any of these factors. I knew the work of missions was challenging. I knew it took funding to make things happen. What I never knew is there are innumerable costs and logistics associated with every missions project, but which can't be put into the monthly newsletter.

After all, everything has a price. Whether it's providing food for the missionary family, putting fuel in the vehicles, paying doctors and lawyers, or hiring a videographer to help tell the story for donors, missions work costs money. Sometimes, you can find people to work for free, but then you're just asking *them* to pay for that which you cannot. Such arrangements are bandages, not solutions, and they often consume inordinate amounts of time, which could be better spent elsewhere.

Time, of course, is something we all have the same amount of. We can't fundraise for extra time. Still, everything has to be organized and managed. From the logistical arrangements for visiting short-term teams, to the hiring of staff, to the feeding schedule for babies or animals, doing good means planning well. With a limited number of hours in the day, and limited funds for staff, sometimes the so-called "real work" - the hands-on part of the job - has to take a back seat.

Remember how I said that many missionaries spend

more time behind a desk than out in the field? What are they doing? They're doing all this stuff - the stuff they can't afford to hire someone else to do. This is why some missionaries cringe at the thought of hosting a team from their church, or of launching their sending pastor's pet project. Because, at the end of the day, they are the ones who have to handle the logistics, the ones who have to manage cost overruns, and the ones stuck footing the bill, financially and relationally, when things go sideways.

So, the next time you have a lightbulb moment and say, "we should...," remember Louise. Recognize that sending money for a new project is not the same as managing that project, that buying materials is not the same as distributing those materials, and that on the other side of your missions effort, someone is struggling to turn your idea into reality. You may have worked hard to raise money and to bring in donated supplies, but it will take additional time, effort, and possibly more money to handle those items on the other side of some massive ocean.

So, cut Louise some slack if she doesn't return your email in a timely manner. Give her a break if her budget numbers don't look like you think they should. Recognize that the cost of doing missions is high, and the missionary, not the donor, is the one paying the real price. If you have questions, ask them, but be prepared to listen and fully process the answers.

Missions work isn't easy and it isn't cheap. Let's ensure that our missions funds aren't given with strings attached. If we trust our friends with the message and work of Jesus in the world, then we should trust them with the financial resources necessary to walk out his mission.

THE SUPPORT NEEDED MOST

TAKE A MOMENT TO think about your life. Think of all the ways you receive personal support from your family, your friends, your church, and other social circles. Think of the financial support you receive from the job you work or from your spouse's job. Think of the spiritual support offered by your local pastor, the emotional support of loving friends, and even the physical support offered by those around you when you find yourself sick, stranded, or lost.

Most of us, if we are honest, will admit that we need every ounce of support we can get. We can't do it all on our own. And sometimes, the casual acquaintance who stops on a rainy day to help us fix a flat tire offers more personal value in that moment than the "good friend" we follow online and get a Christmas card from once a year. Those who make us feel the most supported are those who are the most hands-on with their support.

Which begs the question: How well do we support our missionary friends? Do we send them money each month and forget about them? Maybe we send a team once a year to do a couple of projects. If we're really good, we at least keep in contact with them on a monthly basis. But does that count as true support? Can we provide, from afar, the kind of support they need most? Are we more like the hands-on flat-fixer, or the remote Christmas card sender?

A PATHWAY FOR MISSIONARY LIFE

Most of us, when we think about what it means to support a missionary, think about money. To be sure, missionary work does need to be funded. Additionally, because of work permit restrictions, many missionaries are unable to earn a wage in their host country, meaning they are dependent on funding from supporters. Money is certainly a need, but I've discovered it's not the highest felt need among missionaries.

Another way some people choose to support a missionary is by sending short-term teams to help with projects. The short-term teams who come in and get their hands dirty doing missions work, we suppose, are an incredible asset for a cash-strapped ministry. And though hosting these teams can be a lot of work, I can attest that for some missionaries, they offer a form of much-needed support through relational connection to their sending churches and partners. Still, short-term teams aren't the support needed most.

In fact, what is sorely needed within the missionary community is something all of us need, no matter our location or life situation, but which missionary partners and supporters half a world away simply can't provide. Missionaries need relationships - real, deep, personal relationships. They need other people who are hands-on in their lives, in their ministries, and in their stories.

I was recently speaking to a friend about what it means to have an abundant life. You know, the kind of life spoken of in the bible. And as I wrestled through all the indicators and implications of such a life, I realized that there is a bit of a spectrum upon which we can overlay our lives. On one end is *abundance*. On the other, I determined, is *crisis*.

For those in crisis, they are simply trying to get to something less frantic. They're trying to survive - to reach a point where they know they're going to make it. Survival is the only goal for someone in crisis. "If I can just get through this," they say, "then I can focus on other things."

For those who make it through their crisis and into survival mode, they eventually being to seek something more - stability. It's not enough just to know you're going to make it today. You have to know there's a pathway forward that is sustainable into the future. Someone in survival mode wants nothing more than to come up with a workable plan for the future of their organization and their life. They desperately want to find a way to not slip back into crisis again.

Stability, you see, is a critical component of a life lived well. It's only once you've reached stability in your life that can you truly look toward abundance. It's difficult for someone in survival mode to really embrace and appreciate life. For someone in crisis mode, a life of abundance seems like a distant fantasy - a dream for someone else, but not for me.

So, where do you think most missionaries are on that spectrum?

That's an easy one: Crisis. You may not know this, but many missionaries live each day of their lives on the verge of crisis - financial crisis, emotional crisis, spiritual crisis. What they need is a close group of friends and advisors to help them move from crisis to survival, then onto stability, and ultimately to abundance - not necessarily financial abundance, but the kind of rich life spoken of in scripture.

If there's any one group of people who need to feel God's love every day, to walk in the confidence offered by the Holy Spirit, and to be conscious of the daily offer of grace in their lives, it's missionaries. The work they are doing is hard and thankless and misunderstood. They need to know that God is up to something great and that they get to be part of it.

But how can someone in crisis ever hope to reach that

state of abundance? I can tell you this: walking through that kind of process doesn't work very well over long distances and infrequent meetings. It requires intense focus and consistent presence. It requires "boots on the ground" to befriend, mentor, pastor, and coach missionaries, not on how to run effective ministries, but on how to live the life they are created to live.

So, how do we do that? How does a church in Wichita offer the most needed kind of support to a missionary in Turkey? How can a supporter in Brooklyn even comprehend, let alone offer help to a missionary in Bangkok? Of course, each situation is unique, but here's what I've discovered: without personal, dedicated support, missionaries are likely to fail, to burnout, and to return home feeling defeated.

ON THE GROUND IN KENYA

Here's what we're doing in Kenya. Having seen what burnt out, dejected missionaries look like, and having recognized that long-distance pastoring works about as well as any other kind of long-distance relationship (which is to say, usually not very well), my family made the move to Kenya to become "boots on the ground."

We aren't here to open an orphanage or a center to teach life skills to young mothers. We aren't setting up medical clinics or boarding schools. We're here to do what we know how to do best - to befriend, pastor, and coach - to invest in the lives of people who desperately need someone to invest in them. We're helping the helpers and pouring ourselves into those who are pouring into others.

The church we have launched is known as an "international church," which is an extremely generic way of saying that we endeavor to have people from many countries and cultures in our church community. We already have people from around the world, representing over a dozen different nations, as well as many Kenyans who identify culturally with what we are doing.

In that mix, there are missionaries, relief workers, and even business people who have relocated to Kenya, left family and friends behind, and are now in need of the kind of personal support and understanding that can only be offered by someone in their same shoes, in the same town, and who is dealing with the same cultural adjustments and frustrations. I'm convinced it simply can't happen any other way.

Don't get me wrong, there are many good programs, run by great missions organizations, which are designed to provide some amount of support and encouragement for their missionaries in the field. And they are good at doing what they are designed to do - inform, educate, encourage, and inspire. What they can't do is visit the missionary who is spending a night in jail because they wouldn't pay a bribe. They can't bring tea, a warm blanket, and companionship to the missionary whose power has been out for days. They can't loan a vehicle to a missionary whose wheels just got stolen. In short, they can't be present every day and at a moment's notice.

This is why I believe so strongly in the value of international churches. My job as the pastor of this church is to be consistently present in the lives of the people I pastor, including missionaries, here in Nakuru, Kenya. We're not trying to create a protective bubble to insulate people from the realities of this life. Instead, we're trying to provide the kind of tools they need to navigate the very specific currents of life outside of the more developed western world.

This is not to say we've got it figured out. We don't. We're newbies. But that's the great message I wish I could share with every church and missions organization. You don't have to send cross-cultural veterans to pastor the missionaries and internationals under your care. In fact, it might be good to send someone who can walk hand-in-hand through the struggles, rather than someone who has "been there, done that" and is more prone to dismiss the very real emotions that the missionary is going through.

WE JOURNEY TOGETHER

I'll be honest, there are times when I wonder what I have to offer the missionaries around me. Then, I think of my own pastoral journey. Over the past 15 years, I have had moments when I was at my wits end - when I simply didn't know what else to do or how to handle a situation. And when I sought council from seasoned pastors - that "wise counsel" I've been taught to seek - the advice was most often something like, "It will get better. You'll get through it."

While that's great encouragement for the future, it didn't help me much in the moment, and it didn't offer a practical response to the situation at hand. No, the more helpful responses often came from those who were in the trenches with me, who were experiencing similar issues, and who understood how I was feeling, but could offer a slightly different perspective. They might not have been the wise sages who came through with perfect advice, but they were the ones who helped me put one foot in front of the other and walk through those tough times.

I bring that understanding into this pastoral endeavor in Kenya. I don't have all the answers on how to live an abundant life as a missionary. I am, however, capable of empathy and understanding, and I can ask questions and help process the situation. I can offer a listening ear and an ability to focus and direct the conversation, and I can invite the Holy Spirit to empower that missionary in his or her life.

I can do those things because I'm walking the same road, and I'm persistently present for the people of Nakuru. My prayer is that through our church and personal relationships, we can extend the time our missionary friends are in the field, while also bringing the good news of Jesus to our city.

If I have a friend who is rescuing orphans, caring for

sick moms, or distributing clean water, I want that friend to be doing that work for a long time. If my interaction with them can extend their presence with those in need - for a year, 5 years, or longer - then I can contribute to helping hundreds, possibly thousands, more people.

Sure, the financial support is important, the physical help is appreciated, and the relational connection to the sending church is encouraging, but what is needed most by missionaries around the world is the kind of support which can only be provided locally. That's why I encourage the planting of international churches in the mission field, and why I would challenge churches to support missionaries by sending out people whose primary mission is to provide pastoral support for missionaries.

We simply should not send missionaries out without being willing to support them with the tools they need to do their job effectively. To assume that anyone, no matter how spiritual or mature, could operate at a high level in an international environment without local pastoral support and a local church community is careless at best, and neglectful at worst. To send them out with a mandate to be involved in a local indigenous church, but without understanding the often troublesome realities of such churches, we put them at serious risk in ways we can't begin to comprehend.

We must do better by our missionaries. We must give them the support they need. We must, if necessary, be willing to uproot our lives and offer that support ourselves, in person, on a daily basis.

THE DIFFICULTY OF EMBRACING CULTURE

THE LIFE OF A missionary is not unlike living under water. To be surrounded by the unfamiliar, and suddenly questioning your own survival skills, can be a disorienting and unnerving experience. Like the diver who gives her life over to the SCUBA paraphernalia designed to keep her alive, missionaries are, in many ways, dependent on the expertise and experience of others for their survival.

The necessary funding, the emotional and spiritual support, the relational lifeline to their homeland - all of these allow the missionary to breathe, and to absorb whatever life-giving molecules we all are created to thrive on. But as any diver will tell you, the gear is not the point. All that survival equipment is there for just that - survival.

If the purpose of diving was simply to survive, then there would be no reason to bother getting wet! Breathing, after all, is accomplished quite simply and effectively on dry land - no extra equipment required, no training involved, and with very little risk. Survival can be accomplished out of the water. The point of diving, then, is everything else: the sights, the sounds, and the experience of exploring a world wholly other than your own.

Many divers tell tales of getting lost in that world - of sometimes even embracing the dizzying effects of their alien surroundings, like an out of body experience or a transcendental escape. To fully experience all that the underwater world has to offer, a diver must forget about the gear, and leave behind, if only in short bursts of time, the world of dry land and familiar creatures.

Missionary life is not all that different. Anyone who has ever been to a new country can relate, at least somewhat, to this feeling. If you have ever been to a place that is totally foreign - somewhere completely different than your usual surroundings - then you've experienced this. New sights, sounds, and smells flood your brain in such quantities and at such a rate that you simply can't process everything you're taking in. Sometimes, it's days, weeks, or even months later that your internal processing unit finally catches up - that all the mental images and files have been downloaded and parsed.

The beauty of a holiday or vacation, of course, is that you know you have the ability to file things away and recall them at a later time - that in a week or two, you'll be back home, where you can unpack all that you experienced. Missionaries, however, don't have this luxury. The most they can hope for is a little bit of downtime in their home at the end of the day. There will be no "vacation after the vacation," because they aren't on vacation. There will be no time (at least not soon) when this adventure is over - no time to debrief or unpack. They must process in real-time. And this, I think, is why it can be so difficult to truly embrace a new culture.

DUMPED AT SEA

The diver analogy brings into focus just how unfamiliar a new missions post can be. Some missionaries even enter their new world and new life sight unseen. We would never do that to a diver!

Imagine someone growing up in some landlocked, dusty town, without access to, or any real knowledge of, the sea. Imagine someone who has no more knowledge of the water than most of us have of the Serengeti. Now envision picking that person up in some kind of aircraft, strapping a tank and regulator to their body, and dumping them in the ocean. What would be the result? Would they come back with tales of wonder and amazement? Or would they be so focused on survival that they wouldn't even attempt to take in their surroundings?

The unfortunate truth is that far too many missionaries are dumped at sea by their sending churches and organizations. I've talked to them - people who have lived in a place for decades, but who took several years to even be able to see the beauty around them. I've also watched as newly dumped missionaries struggle for air in their new culture, and as soon as feasible, return to their homeland, washing up on the beach of the familiar, like an uneducated diver gasping for air and grasping for dry ground.

Most new missionaries, I've found, think they can handle this shocking plunge into the unknown. Especially reassured are those who have been on several short-term trips. "I've been there," they think. "I know the culture and the people. I can even speak the language a little bit." But in my own experience, and the experience of countless others, you don't really understand how to live in a place until you're already in over your head.

You see, culture reveals itself gradually. Like diving through a great reef, there are parts of this exciting new world that are immediately visible. There is some amount of beauty that is recognizable at a glance, some level of danger immediately observed. But then there's more…a lot more.

The longer you stay, the more you observe, and the more you explore. As you do, you discover that both the richest beauty and the darkest danger lie beyond the perception of a casual visitor. It is only by venturing into the depths of a place that you truly begin to perceive the full spectrum of a culture.

MAMAW'S BISCUITS

I knew missionaries struggled with their cultural

identity. What I never knew is just how difficult, and perhaps impossible, it is to fully embrace a new culture.

I've often said that culture is sticky. Whatever cultural norms we are surrounded by in our formative years seem to stick with us, even long after we've moved on from them. For example, I grew up in the Southeastern United States. I lived in a fairly rural area with farms all around. In fact, my grandfather, whom I called Papaw, was a cattle farmer, and I spent many weekends and long summer days on his farm.

It was on that small farm that I developed a deep appreciation for the kind of high carb, high fat, high protein meals common to the area. The spreads of food on my grandparents' table were so vast that I sometimes wonder how my grandmother (Mamaw) had time to do anything *besides* cook.

On the farm, it was biscuits, gravy, sausage, eggs, and grits or oatmeal for breakfast. Then, Mamaw's incredible rolls, meatloaf or fried chicken or some other meat, mashed potatoes, gravy, 3 or 4 vegetables, and often some kind of casserole for lunch. Dinner was a lighter fair, by farm standards, but still always consisted of meat, bread, and veggies, with a healthy dose of lard and butter used in the cooking.

This is the food that represents my upbringing - my home. It is my *comfort food*. Even now, a couple of decades later, I still long for those foods. I've never met anyone who can make a biscuit like my grandmother, but I am willing to dive into any reasonably similar disc of doughy, buttery goodness.

Even though I left Tennessee when I was 20 years old, spent time in Ohio, then Texas, and now in Kenya, those old comfort foods still cry out to me. Fortunately, flour is cheap in Kenya. Bacon, however, is not.

Though I've developed a love for many other kinds of food from all around the globe, there is still a special place in my heart and stomach for Mamaw's southern cooking. There are days when the finest cut of kobe beef couldn't compare to a skillet-fried hamburger on white bread with mayo. Why? It's a cultural thing. And culture is sticky.

Food, of course, is important in many cultures around the world. If you ask most people what food they prefer, they will begin to tell you about the food of their homeland. Here in Kenya, when given a choice, most locals will eat ugali (like really stiff grits made with corn flour), sukuma wiki (a type of spinach), or mukimo (mashed potatoes with pumpkin leaves, corn, and other veggies mixed in). Kenyans I know who live in other countries long for this rather bland food the way I long for Mamaw's biscuits.

In this sense, food imitates life. Just as we have difficulty pulling ourselves away from that old home cooking (wherever home may be), we also struggle to pull ourselves away from other cultural norms and comforts. Embracing a culture that is, in some cases, drastically different from our own causes a kind of internal tug-o-war in the depths of our being.

Visiting a place is one thing. Living there is another. There is something inside of us that fears losing our cultural identity. Something else that wants to retreat from the new and run back to the familiar. Yet, for many of us, there is still that adventurous spirit that longs to embrace this vast new world.

All of these emotions racing around inside the mind and body of a missionary can create quite a cultural crucible. I've spoken to missionaries who have lived in the same place for a decade or more who still struggle with their embrace of culture. Some have even abandoned their pursuit of that embrace, and have chosen instead to live in a cultural bubble. Others press on, trying as best they can to become one of the locals - often an impossible mission.

GETTING WET DOESN'T MAKE YOU A FISH

Most missionaries, when they're being honest, will tell you that no matter how hard you try, you will never be a local. You can speak the language, learn the customs, adapt to the lifestyle, but you will always be an outsider. Like the beloved pet who thinks he's a person, you might convince yourself that you're just part of the family or community, but it turns out that cultural immersion doesn't make you native any more than getting wet makes you a fish. There seems to always be lurking, just around the corner, an event or circumstance that reminds you and those around you that something about you is different.

For one missionary friend, that difference became very apparent when violence erupted in the country where he was working. As Lee explained it to me, "The biggest difference between me and my co-workers, me and my flatmates, me and my friends, was that I had a U.S. Passport, and within minutes, I could book a flight out of the turmoil…and they all knew it."

Lee could escape the danger. In a couple of days, he could fly back to a place with row houses and delicious bratwursts, instead of rockets and malicious bombs. His friends would be left behind, unable to flee from those who sought to destroy them. Ultimately though, he stayed.

He stayed and helped his friends, encouraging them, sheltering them. But even then, he still knew he was different. *They* still knew he was different. Every day, one of his friends asked him if he was going to leave. Every day, he told them he was staying. And every day, he knew they weren't asking that question of anyone else. Only *he* had the option of getting out.

Embracing culture, then, might be a fools errand. Appreciating it, exploring it, experiencing it - all of these are within the grasp of the missionary. In fact, they should all be part of the missionary life. But what if we gave our missionaries a pass on the idea that they have to "live like the locals?" What if we allowed that there will always be a cultural dissonance in their lives? And what if we determined not to dismiss that struggle, but to learn about it, to understand it. What if we worked to find a good dive master to help them navigate these strange, beautiful waters?

You see, there's more to embracing culture than eating weird foods and learning new languages. To fully embrace a new place, you would have to go much further than anyone has ever gone before. To live in this world, you would have to learn to swim without the SCUBA gear - to breathe underwater. You would have to grow gills and fins - to become something other than what you are. That's the impossible task that we often expect of our missionary friends, rather than expending the time, energy, and resources to properly equip them for the underwater adventure of a lifetime.

WHAT I DIDN'T KNOW I DIDN'T KNOW

IT WAS FEBRUARY 12, 2002, just five months after the attacks of September 11, 2001 on New York City and Washington, D.C. The evidence of Iraqi WMDs (and of their involvement in the attacks) was shaky at best. The White House was facing tough criticism about their justification for war in the Middle East, and it was Donald Rumsfled's job to assure the public that they hadn't gotten it wrong.

Rumsfeld attempted to put into perspective the difficult task at hand when, during a U.S. Department of Defense news briefing, he said these infamous words:

"Reports that say that something hasn't happened are

always interesting to me, because as we know, there are known knowns; there are things we know we know. We also know there are known unknowns; that is to say we know there are some things we do not know. But there are also unknown unknowns -- the ones we don't know we don't know. And if one looks throughout the history of our country and other free countries, it is the latter category that tend to be the difficult ones."

*   - U.S. Secretary of Defense, Donald Rumsfeld*

His response to the criticism, to be honest, didn't answer the questions people had raised. It was, however, an accurate assessment of the situation in the Middle East in 2002. People wanted specifics. Rumsfeld gave them generalities. They wanted evidence. He gave them philosophy.

But it was good philosophy. Though the English language may have failed Rumsfeld in its lack of properly descriptive words, the point he attempted to make is incredibly valid, and actually, he articulated it about as well as possible.

As linguist Geoffrey K. Pullum explained in his defense of Rumsfeld's statement, "The quotation is impeccable, syntactically, semantically, logically, and rhetorically. There is nothing baffling about its language at all." The truth expressed in the statement is even less baffling. The idea that there are unknown unknowns - things "we don't know we don't know" - applies to essentially everything we put our minds to.

Even purported experts in a given field will admit that not only are there questions they have yet to find answers to, but that there are questions they haven't even thought to ask. Some of the most animated moments in science have been punctuated by an observation or finding that the scientific researcher wasn't looking for, didn't expect, or hadn't considered.

Often, the more we learn, the more questions we have. For this reason, so-called experts are often the most confused about a subject. Novices can throw out answers and theories about everything, but informed, educated analysis often causes us to not only reject our "common sense" assumptions, but to begin asking entirely different sets of questions.

The father of modern genetics, Gregor Mendel, didn't set out to prove a theory about dominant and recessive genes. Instead, in researching how traits were passed on from parent to offspring in pea plants, he discovered certain ratios of those traits that led him to ask a different set of questions.

Scottish biologist Alexander Fleming went on vacation in the fall of 1928, and upon return to his lab, discovered an unusual fungus growing on one of his cultures - a fungus that had completely killed off all surrounding bacteria. That fungus? Penicillin. Sometimes the things we discover accidentally are just as important as, or more important than, what we set out to find.

WE KNOW NEXT TO NOTHING

The unknown unknowns - what we don't know we don't know - comprise the largest subset of all knowledge. In fact, some scientists estimate that the percentage of knowable knowledge that is currently known (got that?) is hovering below 1%. In other words, of all the possible things that one could learn in the universe, right now, the combined knowledge of everyone who has ever lived equals somewhere just north of *nothing*. That leaves a lot yet to discover!

But most of us don't operate this way. Most of us don't assume that we know next to nothing - less than 1% of what there is to be known. Typically, we estimate our knowledge, or at least our ability to ask the right questions, at some much higher percentage. For every Alexander Fleming, who studied that strange fungus, there are likely thousands of others who would have, literally or figuratively, simply thrown out the sample.

When it comes to missions work, I've discovered that not only are there scores of questions I want answered, but that there is some nearly infinite number of questions I haven't even thought to ask. In seeking answers to one set of questions, I realized there were whole topics I had never considered. In most cases, I began hearing and observing the *answers* long before I ever began to formulate the *questions*. Like Mendel, my missionary pea plants started turning out a little funky, so I attempted to figure out why.

That's not to say that what follows is some exploration of uncharted waters. Much of what I didn't know I didn't know was, nonetheless, known by *someone*. I have, in my study and research, come across a small minority of people who have been seeking answers to some of these questions for decades.

You may read something here and say, "I've been talking about that for years." That's great! I'm glad! Keep talking about this stuff, because it is vital to the survival of our missionary friends, and to the work of the Kingdom of God. I am grateful for those who have begun to delve into the deeper questions of missions and relief work, and I hope many more jump on board.

Some of the items discussed here are ones we should have been thinking and talking about from the beginning. Others are unique in our modern era. But in all cases, what I didn't know I didn't know has had a profound and lasting effect on me as a supporter and pastor of missionaries. I cannot unsee these things, cannot unring these bells. I cannot ignore them.

ANSWERS IN THE FORM OF A QUESTION

So, what were these unknown unknowns? For me, in my limited perspective on missions, some things I had never considered were how human nature and human assumptions intersect with sacred work. What happens when a group of people set out to do what's right, but can't agree on just how to proceed? What happens when well-meaning people truly muck it up and leave behind a situation far worse than when they started?

How do people from different parts of the world, living

in different cultures and places and separated by multiple timezones, ever find a way to effectively communicate with each other? What are the expectations placed on them - from outsiders, insiders, and themselves - which drive them, and at times, consume and overwhelm them?

These are the questions I'll explore here. They are questions I began to ask after watching missionary friends implode, after seeing the effects of missions gone wrong, and after attempting to wrap my head around what it means to be a fallible human being doing the work of the divine in a very broken world.

They are the tip of a very large iceberg - the indicators of just how far I have to go in my knowledge of missions and missionaries. There are still a whole host of unknown unknowns out there, and I stumble over them, crash into them, and become undone by them on a regular basis.

But I'm learning that's not such a bad thing. It keeps me sharp. It keeps me focused. It keeps me on the lookout for those discoveries, great and small, which will help equip missionaries, educate churches, and propel the mission of God in the world.

THE MISSIONARY COMPETITION

WHY IS IT THAT human beings turn everything into a competition? Why do we view the failures and successes of others in light of our own successes and failures? When a colleague loses 40 pounds, instead of celebrating with him, we get irked about our own failed attempts at weight loss. When our sister gets a promotion at work, we grumble about how deserving we are of a professional upgrade. When our friend's kid makes honor roll or takes first place at the swim meet, we are quick to point out how smart and talented our own kids are - not in an effort to reassure our offspring, but in an attempt to inspire, or at least console, ourselves.

Let's face it, we all want to win. We want to be the best at whatever we set our mind to. We want to reap the rewards of our efforts. If, in that process, someone else has to go down, then so be it. It is, after all, survival of the fittest.

Except it's not. Or at least, it *shouldn't* be. One of the biggest problems God seems to see with our broken world is our "winner take all" attitude. In his time on earth, Jesus regularly shot down the idea of striving to be number one. In fact, he flipped everything on its head with his "last will be first" and "blessed are the meek" talk. We know this, and yet we find ourselves competing over everything - trivial things like Little League prowess and important things like relationships, church, and yes, missions.

I never knew missionaries were so competitive. My impression of missionaries had always been that they were a pretty humble and genteel lot. Having given up many of the comforts and conveniences of their former life, surely the posture of a missionary was more akin to Jesus washing his disciples' feet than it was to those arrogant disciples jockeying for position in the Kingdom of God. But I was wrong.

This competitive streak is no secret among missionaries. In fact, nearly every missionary I talk to tells me about how competitive *other* missionaries are. (The fact is not lost on me that a self-aggrandizing perspective makes it easy to point fingers at others.) So, what's all this missionary competition about anyway?

CLASH FOR CASH

First, it's about finances. As I said before, it costs a lot of money to do good, and most missionaries are stretched pretty thin. Even those who are excellent money managers often find themselves scraping the bottom of the financial barrel in order to execute their vision. Charitable donations are down across the board, and there just doesn't seem to be enough money to go around. There is, to be frank, a scarcity mentality among many in the missionary community, and the fear and anxiety produced by that scarcity mentality drives missionaries into a "cash competition" mindset.

Fortunately, this one is easily combatted. For one, you could send more money to your missions partners. You might be surprised how little they would actually need in order to reduce their financial anxiety. For a church to find an extra $100 per month in the budget is typically not that difficult. But in a country where $100 could feed a family for 3 months, or send two children to school for a year, that hundred bucks is vital.

Every missionary I know needs more resources, and I would guess that for most, a 10-20% increase in their monthly income would be enough to help them sleep better at night. So, how can you help fight against competition for cash in the missionary community? Give more. Start by increasing your giving by 10% and encourage others to do the same. Your missionary partners will thank you.

In fact, do that now. Put down this book and go give what you can (plus a little more) to your missionary friend. Tell them I told you to. Trust me, they will appreciate the unexpected gift.

Did you do it? OK. Welcome back.

Money isn't the only driver of competition among missionaries. In fact, money is the easy one. It's the one that can be fixed. You can literally throw money at that problem and make it go away!

FIGHTING FOR WHAT IS RIGHT

The second driver of competition among missionaries is much more difficult to combat, because it's a philosophical one. You see, just as almost all of us are competitive, we are also all convinced we are right. We are convinced that our way is the best way, or at least that we're heading down the right path. We might even find a small community of people committed to that same path with whom we can connect.

The trouble comes when someone else pops onto the scene with a different idea or method and begins to stir the pot within our little group. This happens among missionaries all the time.

I was first made aware of these intertribal divides by Lacy, a long-time missionary in the Middle East. Within Lacy's circle of missionary friends (who all had to operate covertly in their city) were teachers, business people, church planters, relief workers, and healthcare professionals.

The teachers felt strongly that education, opportunity, and personal relationship were the key drivers of missions in that region. The business people agreed - sort of. For them, opportunity was number one, regardless of education, and relationships were within the context of business.

The relief workers and healthcare pros were similar to each other in their desire to meet the physical needs of the people. The common refrain within their circle was that it's hard for someone to be hungry for God if they are hungry for food, or that people won't listen to how God wants to heal their heart until you heal their body. They saw themselves as modern day expressions of Jesus' miracles - healing the sick, feeding the poor, helping the outcast.

The church planters turned their noses up at all the other groups, convinced that church planting is the only real missions work. The other do-gooders were taking the safe path, not walking in faith and trusting in God for safety and provision. Church planting, they self-assuredly explained, is *pure* missions work, not cloaked in language of education or healthcare or relief, and not funded by grants and private corporations. Their work, they reasoned, was the kind of work the Apostle Paul involved himself in, even when faced with persecution.

According to Lacy, there were maybe two dozen missionaries in her city - two dozen people who had similar stories of dropping everything and moving to a war zone for the sake and cause of Jesus. But among these two dozen missionaries, there were all these divisions. The teachers mostly kept to themselves, the business development people didn't talk to the humanitarians, and worst of all were the "CPs" - the high and mighty church planters - who only seemed to want to talk to people who could help them in some way.

What was the genesis of these divisions? It couldn't have been that one group didn't think the other was doing any good. Each group had ample evidence of the positive impact they were making in the city. Likewise, the division wasn't caused by a disagreement in theology. All were fairly mainline in their beliefs. No, the major difference between these groups was a philosophical one.

Each group had a different answer to a simple question: "What is the best way to do missions?"

Driven by their need to be right, each of these groups had circled the wagons with their own kind, united in their disdain for the others, and formed little cliques that liked to pat each other on the back, while criticizing those who chose (or were called by God) to do missions differently.

So, here we had 25 people, splintered into groups of 6 or 7, grumbling about each other rather than working together toward common goals. What a great picture of God's Kingdom! What a great example for those they were trying to reach with the good news of Jesus! The question is, how do we solve this problem?

TOWARD UNIFICATION

In my experience, there are two things that bring disparate groups together. The first is a *unifying negative experience*. The second is a simple change in operating philosophy.

A unifying negative experience is typically imposed by an outside force - a tragedy, threat, or other event that causes people to lay down their differences and unite in opposition to something larger. The terrorist attacks of September 11, 2001 did this in the U.S., especially in New York City, where people from across the spectrum of socio-economic and ethnic groups came together in unprecedented acts of unity, rallying against an ominous outside threat.

In Lacy's case, this is exactly what happened among the missionaries in her city. As the local government began to clamp down on Christian religious activity, the 25 missionaries discovered a bond in their similarities - persecution tends to do that. When faced with threats of death, the small community united in an effort to press forward with God's work in their city. When someone needed to hide from the authorities for a day or a week, they weren't picky about who provided the hiding place. A unifying negative experience broke down the barriers that divided these groups.

The other way of bringing together cliquish groups is perhaps more effective in the long run, but requires a much more deliberate approach. That is, there has to be a change in operating philosophy - a fundamental rewriting of the question everyone is seeking to answer. This type of change is also often imposed by an outside force, but could jut as easily be driven by one or more people *within* the community who have a desire to see unity in the ranks.

To see unity, especially long-term, in these kinds of groups, we must move beyond the question of "What is the best way to do missions?" Instead, we have to ask questions like, "How can all of these approaches work together for a greater good?" Rather than passing judgment on the approach of others, we must accept their approach, flawed though we may view it, and look for ways to complement it - ways to add value to the work they are doing. We must ask questions and seek to learn from them about their way of doing things.

In other words, instead of assuming they don't know what they're doing, or that they are inferior, we change our assumptions. We assume that they know something we don't know, that they have something to teach us, and that we, if we are willing to learn, can become better at walking out our own calling by being around them.

This kind of unity is what much of my own work is driving toward. I'm saddened when I sit down with missionary after missionary who feel like they are misunderstood or looked down upon. "Everybody else is so competitive and judgmental," is the common refrain in the missionary community. However, for a pastor like myself, there is a silver lining to this cloud. If everyone hates the constant in-fighting and competition (even if they are unknowingly contributing to it) then there's hope for a brighter tomorrow.

Part of my job is to help build bridges within the missionary community. My chosen method is to create a church environment where differences are embraced and discussion encouraged - where we're less concerned about proving how right we are and more concerned with growing closer to Jesus and to walking out the calling he has for us individually and collectively.

I look forward to the day when the tide turns in the missionary community and missionaries all realize that we are not in competition with each other, that we are all on the same team, and that God has the ability to provide vision, energy, and resources for all of us in the way he sees fit. May the God who has ordained such diversity in the work of missions also speak to the hearts of his workers.

THE SIDE-EFFECTS OF MISSIONS WORK

IF IT'S TRUE THAT there are two sides to every story, then missionaries and their partners back home have to be prepared for the ugly "other side" of all the missions success stories we've heard and shared. It would be nice if this weren't the case. We want to believe there's no downside to all this perceived good. In truth, we know the news can't all be good, even though that is typically the only variety we hear from the font lines of missions.

Occasionally, some bad news gets through. We've all

heard of kids dying of curable diseases because of a lack of supplies or equipment. We've seen pictures of villages burned because their inhabitants were too weak or too small in number to fight off local warlords. We understand that help doesn't always arrive in time, and that sometimes it's too little, too late.

We know these things happen in developing nations, and we surmise that we must do more. After all, many of these tragedies could be averted or mitigated if there was more help available. These are the side-effects of a plentiful harvest, but too few workers.

What most of us don't know, and what I never knew, is that missions work itself often has side-effects - that the downside of missions isn't only about what we *can't* do, but is sometimes about what we manage *to* do. Often, when we flip the coin on those missions success stories, we find something disturbing on the other side: a tale of people who meant well, but caused great harm. The side-effects of missions work, I have learned, are complex, far-reaching, and very macro, but are still felt every day by local workers, villagers, businesses, and even missionaries themselves.

WE KNOW NOT WHAT WE DO

In her 2009 book *Dead Aid: Why Aid Is Not Working and How There Is a Better Way for Africa*, Zambian-born author Dambisa Moyo argues that western aid policies, and the accompanying aid dependency of recipient nations, has done more to harm developing economies than it has to bolster them. She garnered much attention by suggesting that the best way to help African countries and other aid recipients is to cut them off - to set an end date for all foreign aid.

While many disagree with Moyo's conclusion, and some may argue against some of her finer points, very few people who have been involved with work in the developing world can argue with the fact that though trillions of dollars in aid money has been directed at developing nations, most of those nations are no better for it. In fact, some are far worse off than they were 50 years ago.

The loudest and most persuasive arguments against Moyo have been that, by calling for the elimination of all foreign aid, she's throwing the baby out with the bath water. There aren't many convincing arguments that the water itself doesn't need to go. International aid and development is, by most accounts, broken and in need of repair.

In Kenya, for example, the evidence is clear that western influence - both from international aid organizations and from missionaries - has had certain unintended side-effects on the culture. For their part, many missionaries and relief workers on the ground know this and are trying to do something about it, but reversing course on this moving locomotive can be hard.

So, what are these negative side-effects of missions in the world? As Moyo points out, dependency of any sort, if fostered in a perpetual way, tears at the fabric of society. We know this. We apply this knowledge in other areas of our lives. We talk about it in parenting courses, counseling sessions, and business lectures. Eventually, a person, a business, a government, or an entire society has to learn to stand on its own two feet. But some in the missionary community, especially historically, have done a poor job of thinking about the long-term societal effects of their short-term programs.

CAUTIONARY TALES

Imagine a clean water initiative that distributes water filters to rural parts of Uganda. We'll call it "Water4U". Like many clean water projects, Water4U is very successful at raising the necessary funds and distributing their chosen type of filter - a portable charcoal-based unit. They tug at the heartstrings of donors with pictures of muddy water and children with bloated bellies and flies on their forehead, and they turn those donated dollars into a valuable service for rural people in desperate need of clean drinking water.

This is a noble effort. There's no corruption in their ranks, no overspending on frivolous projects. By just about any measure, Water4U is an example of how to do missions right. Their success is hailed on their website and in their monthly newsletters. Their donors go to bed at night knowing they've helped to bring clean, healthy water to thousands. So, what's the problem?

There are a few. First off, Water4U is using a filter that lasts for about a year of regular use. That's a great gift to give - a full year of clean drinking water. But then what?

At the end of that year, is there anyone around to replenish those filters, or have they moved on to other villages and cities? Let's face it, donors like to hear about another 100 villages receiving clean water. They tend to want *more people* to be helped, rather than the *same people* to be helped more.

But even if there is a system in place to replace the filters, the truth is, unless the filter distribution is accompanied by clean water education, those filters may not have been used at all. In many scenarios like this, the locals see much more value in having a couple of new buckets (primary components of most filter systems) than they do in the filter itself. So, the adoption of the valuable filters is an uphill climb.

Even the best-case scenario here is that the representatives from Water4U show up a year later, drop off more filters, hop back in their Landcruisers, and head off to save someone else's day. Hail the conquering heroes! These needy people now have clean water, but they are completely dependent on the western missionary to provide it.

The replacement filters, imported from some far away land, are not accessible to the people who need them. Even if they were, they are far too expensive for the poorest of the poor. For these people, their survival depends on the missionary. No missionary, no clean water, no life. This is the product of a good idea done bad, and it's not an uncommon story.

Meanwhile, in the cities, another side-effect has reared its head. The abundance of "Clothes for Africa" drives back in the U.S. has resulted in an influx of second-hand clothes, carefully curated from the overstuffed closets of suburban Americans. These clothes are processed by a multi-national aid organization and shipped to parts unknown.

Upon arrival in their destination country, the clothes are bundled and sold - yes, *sold* - to local shop-owners, who, in turn, sell them on the streets for pennies. The resultant lowered cost of clothing has put local clothing retailers, manufacturers, and textile mills out of business. Thousands of vulnerable people have lost jobs, while Americans say with pride, "I gave my clothes to some poor kid in Africa."

To exacerbate the problem, there is now no going back. Even if all the second-hand clothes stopped flowing in, those shuttered factories wouldn't have the capital to reopen. And even if they did manage to find such capital, they wouldn't have the skilled workers to make the fabric and clothes. Likewise, local people, having now allocated their funds for other uses, wouldn't have the financial flexibility to afford the new, more expensive clothing.

In short, a group of well-meaning people managed to kill an entire industry and put thousands of people out of work. This is not a theory, this is the harsh reality in many parts of the world. Here in Kenya, a once-booming textile industry has been largely shuttered. And now that we've created this mess, we have to feed the machine by continuing to provide clothes for those "poor kids in Africa."

This knowledge has completely changed my perspective on foreign aid. Every time I see a kid wearing a Boston Marathon '08 cap or a Camp Winnetauka t-shirt, I'm reminded of the unintended consequences of our actions - the side-effects of well-meaning missions work.

CREATING VIABLE ALTERNATIVES

So, on one hand, we create poorly-conceived projects, raise money, then abandon people. On the other hand, we ride in on our white horse with a savior complex, and leave behind a people wholly dependent on our assistance for their survival. It's no wonder that some countries are now actively discouraging missionary involvement - not for religious reasons, but for the welfare of their people.

But there is another way. Within the missionary community, many are sitting up and taking notice at the impact they are making. Individual missionaries and missions organizations around the world have made dramatic changes to the way they operate. No longer can we "do good" in a bubble. We must take into account the social, economic, environmental, and cultural impact of our actions, and create programs that are viable, and ultimately, self-sustaining.

We must not only do good in the short-term, but we must consider the long-term ramifications of our actions. We must seek to end the cycle of dependence and move toward independence, and even abundance, for those we seek to help.

To borrow and twist a phrase: Give a man a free shirt, and he'll be clothed for a day. Teach him how to sew a shirt, and he'll be clothed for a lifetime, have a viable business, provide for his family, and employ many others.

The side-effects of missions work have, in many places, been much more detrimental than the work has been beneficial. We are operating at a net loss, and we need to right the ship, mixaphorically speaking.

I am fortunate to have good friends who are committed to righting that ship, and they are doing so by working toward sustainable efforts. One friend is creating a water filter that will last well over a decade, and hopes to one day be able to employ local people in the manufacture of that filter - a clean water solution designed in Africa, manufactured in Africa, for Africa. Other friends have invested their time, efforts, and not a small sum of money, into rekindling the garment, textile, and fashion industries in Kenya.

One friend, who is working to provide necessary capital to fuel healthy business development across the continent of Africa, put it bluntly. He said, "Look, I'm a businessman. All I know how to do is business. Why would I move to some far-away land and build an orphanage or start a water project? I don't know anything about those. What I do is invest in businesses, and help people learn how to grow their business so that they don't have to face the choice of whether or not to abandon their baby. I invest in businesses so that people can earn enough money to *afford* a water filter." Does he "count" as a missionary? In my book, he certainly does.

These friends, and the organizations they represent, understand that healthy missionary work leads to healthy people and a healthy society. They operate under the assumption that the gospel of Jesus should bring good news, not only spiritually, but physically as well. They appreciate that any missional effort should include an exit strategy - that those receiving assistance should have a clear pathway toward independence.

If the church and the missionaries we send out are doing our job well, those we touch will be left with a better life. They should be reliant on God, not on the missionary. They should recognize that the good news of Jesus is for here and now, not just for after they die. Anything less just has too many side-effects.

THE COMPLEXITIES OF COMMUNICATION

IT WAS 1:00 on a peaceful Tuesday afternoon, and I had a question. It wasn't an urgent question, but in an attempt to offload my mental plate, I aimed to ask it. As I've done for most of my working life, I fired off an email to a colleague and awaited a response. None came. Hours went by. Then days. Then weeks. Still no response.

I began to wonder if my correspondence had gotten tucked behind an old shelf in the mailroom of the world wide web. Perhaps a digital dog ate it. (I suspected that crazy Firefox or his terrorizing big brother, Mozilla.) What happened? This was someone I interacted with on a regular basis, someone with whom I worked on dozens of projects when I was back in the U.S., so why the radio silence now?

Several weeks later, I had a video chat with my friend, and in the midst of our conversation, I casually asked if he had received my email. "Oh yes, I've been meaning to reply to that," was his response. Again, this was very out of character for this individual. I was determined to discover the reason for his delay, but didn't want to make him feel more awkward, so I looked to myself instead.

Surely there was something I had done to cause or contribute to his lack of response. Maybe I said something offensive. Perhaps I asked a question that required him to research the answer before responding. Had I been unclear about my desire for a response? Surely there was something I was missing.

Then it hit me. I had sent the email at 1:00 in the afternoon local time - a reasonable time of day to expect a response. Except I live in Kenya and my friend lives in Texas. The email came through at 4:00am his time.

Though he's a notoriously early riser, chances are he was still in bed, sound asleep when my note arrived.

Then, if he's like most people, he woke up, took a shower, got ready for work, had a cup of coffee, and headed out to the office. Once he arrived at work, he checked his email to find 10 items that needed immediate attention, and two new meetings he needed to schedule. My email, falling somewhere in the midst of all the others, wasn't as urgent as his work correspondence. After all, his company puts food on the table for his family!

He probably glanced at my note, determined to revisit it later, and went on with his day. Of course, it's easy for an email to get buried over the course of a day or two. Nearly everyone has done what my friend did and forgotten to return to an older email and reply. I don't blame him.

THE IMPORTANCE OF "WHEN"

What dawned on me - what I already knew, but had somehow forgotten - is that in our fast-paced, always-on, email-driven world, the "when" really matters. Businesses know this. They will spend thousands of dollars trying to determine the precise moment to send email marketing campaigns. They study to see when their target audience is online, when they are most receptive to the marketing message, and even when they are most likely to forward something to a friend. The "when" is of utmost importance.

I do this, too. All of my mass email correspondence is scheduled to hit inboxes as optimal times, but I failed to apply the same strategy to my more personalized correspondence. With my email to my friend, I missed his "when." My message got to him at a time when he was least likely to see it and least likely to respond. (It doesn't take thousands of dollars in research to figure that out!)

Likewise, many emails that come to me from the west miss *my* "when." I often receive emails at midnight local time with someone expecting a quick reply. Sometimes it even takes me days to respond, as the email gets buried in my inbox. I'm sure I have disappointed people, many times over, just like my friend disappointed me, and it's all because our "whens" are out of alignment.

While phone and internet technology has done much to improve our communication, our reliance on these forms of instant access has created the expectation that everyone is available all the time. We are used to sending messages from our phone, or being able to video chat at a moment's notice. Talking to a missionary, then, who is five, eight, or twelve time zones away can quickly become a chore, and as such, can easily fall by the wayside.

WORTH THE EFFORT

Of course, it's not only the time difference that interferes with communication between missionaries and their partners. Internet reliability issues, cultural dissonance, and many other factors serve to disrupt what should be a solid and consistent flow of information back and forth between those attempting to do the difficult work of missions and the people who are trying to support them. While this may be a minor issue to the church missions pastor or missionary supporter, it can sometimes feel like death for the missionary.

One of the primary difficulties of missionary life, and one of the key drivers of missionary burnout, is the feeling of isolation. When we stop communicating, or fail to communicate well, those feelings become more intense. By being unwilling to work through the communication challenges with our missionary friends, we very often reinforce the common missionary refrain, "I feel like everyone has forgotten about me."

Over the years, I've heard many stories of churches and supporters who were offended because a missionary hasn't kept in touch. "Sure," they say, "I get the email newsletters, but would it be such a burden to send a personal note now and then?"

My answer, of course, is that email works both ways. If you want to hear about how life is going in Angola, make the effort to contact your friend there. Consider the math: for you to reach out to your missionary friend requires 5 minutes of your time to send one email. However, for your missionary friend to make personal contact with every individual and church supporter (which would be required to facilitate personal communication without offense), could require hours or even days of time, sending dozens or hundreds of emails.

While it may be advisable for missionaries to take the time for such correspondence, it is a hefty expectation. Much more manageable would be the expectation that the missionary simply reply to the personal correspondence from others - something most missionaries are happy to do.

So, though it may be hard work, it is truly the responsibility of those on the "sending" side (the church, organization, family, and friends) to invest in this type of communication. In my experience, most missionaries assume that if you don't reach out to them, you probably don't want to talk. So take the first step and find a way to establish regular communication with your missionary friends. Trust me, they will be thrilled to hear from you.

A FAILURE TO COMMUNICATE

Of course, email correspondence and personal contact from "back home" are incredibly important for missionaries, but such interaction is only one area of necessary missionary communication. There are many other people with whom missionaries are required to communicate on a regular basis.

The modern missionary is expected to relate well with local and state government officials, with staff and organizational leaders, with other missionaries and missions organizations, with local pastors and church leadership, and the list goes on.

Missionary life is full of complex communication, and

many missionaries struggle to communicate well with their many contacts. The missionaries I talk to want to communicate and cooperate, but don't know where to start. To be honest, very few of them have the relational ability, time, or energy to invest in such an endeavor, so they simply go about their business, wishing someone else would reach out to them.

A typical conversation with my missionary friends involves some lament about how different missionaries and missions organizations fail to work together. In fact, even missionaries who are working in the same area, with the same people, often fail to communicate. Sometimes, they don't even know the other exists. Everyone, it seems, is staying in their own lane with their head down - hard at work, but oblivious to others.

You see, most missionaries are hands-on people. They like to do stuff. They like to take action. Many are also visionaries, with big dreams and a knack for seeing the big picture. Very few are planners, organizers, or natural communicators. They might be able to speak to a crowd, but few have the skills necessary to organize a meeting of like-minded people or to build coalitions between organizations.

Not coincidentally, those who do possess these relational skills find that their work is greatly enhanced by the partnerships they create. They are able to work together with others to fill in the gaps in their expertise, able to pool resources with others to pull off larger projects, and to tap into larger networks in ways that further their work.

Meanwhile, the majority of missionaries struggle along, alone and isolated in their work. But this doesn't have to be. When I talk to missionaries and hear their concerns, I realize there can be a new way forward, if only we're willing to forge that path.

A HOLISTIC APPROACH

Imagine what would happen if we prioritized our communication - if we were determined to do communication well. What would happen if churches and missions organizations resolved from the start to do missions work in partnership and communication not only with one missionary or one local organization, but with several missionaries and several organizations within the same city or region?

What if instead of seeing a need and addressing it (which, on the surface, sounds like a very noble endeavor), we focused our missions efforts on identifying a need and then trying to find others who are already attempting to address that need. What if we determined to listen to people already on the ground before sending out a missionary to start something afresh?

This is all part of the communications process. We listen, research, visit, learn from others, and then try to fill in the gaps and provide the necessary support. Part of the reason there are so many people trying to do the same kind of work in the same places is that no one is taking the time to communicate. We aren't doing the hard work of communication before investing the time, energy, and resources in our missions endeavors.

It's time we stop reinventing the wheel in missions. It's time to humble ourselves and to learn from others - to ask questions rather than only offering answers. It's time to do the hard work of communication and to equip our missionary friends to do the same.

I believe the results of such an effort would be deeply felt and long-lasting. Our missionary friends would feel supported and encouraged, leading to longer engagements and less burnout. Our projects would be better-informed and backed by more resources as we tap into local and trans-local networks.

Our collective missions knowledge would be boosted, as we begin to build upon the work of others, rather than always starting from the ground up. Most importantly, God's purposes in the world would be served in a more efficient and effective manner.

We serve a God who values communication so much that he came to earth and put on flesh and allowed people to talk to him face to face. We serve a God who desires communication so much that he has given us an open line directly to him through prayer. We serve a God who wants so badly to communicate with us that he has sent the Holy Spirit to speak to us in deeply personal ways.

If we are to walk out his mission in the world, we must learn to place the same value on communication as does the God we serve.

THE EXPECTATIONS GAME

IT'S 10:45AM WHEN Andy takes the stage at Grace Community Church. His stomach is in knots and he's sure that if he had eaten anything that morning, he wouldn't be able to keep it down. He's a guy who has faced interrogation by tribal chiefs and intimidation by police chiefs, he's eaten strange bugs, contracted strange bugs, and once, even had his phone bugged. Speaking in front of 500 missionary-loving church people shouldn't cause such a visceral reaction.

Yet, here he is - barely able to make his way onto the stage. His host makes the introduction and the crowd applauds, just as others have done at the half dozen churches he's visited in the past month. They are eager to hear about his adventures, about the work of his organization, and about how much of an impact their missions dollars are having.

His presentation is polished. His slides are prepared. Still, as he takes the stage and begins to speak, all Andy can hear is the parting shot from his wife Claire, spoken only an hour earlier. "Go ahead, smile and lie. I can't do it anymore." He wonders what exactly she can't do anymore. Was she just talking about this presentation, or was there more? Is she done with their missions work? Done with their marriage?

Whatever the case, he knows he has to get that out of his mind for now. There are 500 people waiting for him to say something, and they have certain expectations...

UNEXPECTED HONESTY

The expectations game is the cause of mountains of anxiety for many missionaries. If you ask most missions partners, they'll tell you they don't really have stringent expectations of the missionaries they support. They'll tell you about the great work being done by missionaries, and that they're just trying to be supportive. But if you ask the missionaries, they tell a different story.

The darkest days of missionaries are filled with the echoes of expectation. The locals they serve have expectations about what the missionary should be providing. Their fellow missionaries expect them to follow some unwritten code of conduct. Their non-missionary expat friends seem to expect them to act different enough to be noticed, but still not be weird.

Their friends and family back home expect them to write and video chat often to give them updates that are full of excitement and short on the mundane details. Partner churches want letters, blog posts and well-produced videos (two minutes or less) to show their congregations. After all, it's important to stay in front of the donors!

What nobody expects, it seems, is for missionaries to be human. Nobody expects them to have bad days. Nobody expects them to struggle spiritually, emotionally, or relationally.

Several months ago, I wrote a very honest blog post in which I tried to explain some of the same struggles and realities expressed in this book. It was a reflection on dozens of very frank conversations with my missionary friends, and a response to how my eyes had been opened to the difficulties of missionary life. I wanted others to see what I had seen. I wanted them to step back and realize that missionaries are real people with real lives, not perfect saints, displayed like statues behind glass cases.

The response I received from a small minority of people confirmed the worst fears of my missionary friends. People actually *are* judging them for being human. Here's a sample.

"Sounds like he needs to come home…"

"Just goes to show how low down and sneaky these missionaries are."

"Ungrateful."

"…it's a [blog post] from someone who does not know God."

Fortunately, these types of responses made up less than 5% of all the comments, but it only takes one comment like that from a supposed friend to send a missionary back into her shell.

While those negative responses got my blood boiling, the ones that compelled me to write this book were the hundreds from missionaries and others who said things like:

"Spot on!"

"I thought I was the only one who felt this way."

And the kicker: *"I have never heard this much honesty from a Christian."*

That one came like a punch to the gut. Honesty should be a hallmark of what it means to be a follower of Jesus. Yet we know from experience that many Christians, especially those in official ministry roles, fail the authenticity test time and time again.

Most people assume there is some moral flaw in these people. Surely they set out to be hypocrites. But what I've found is that the lack of authenticity among pastors and missionaries usually comes down to this: they are trying their best to live up to the expectations of others, and at times, their own expectations of themselves.

They struggle to reconcile the lofty expectations of others with their own ideals of authenticity and transparency. Constantly battle these two opposing forces, they sometimes begin to live double-lives - lying to themselves and others, and concealing the truth from everyone.

THE TRUTH BEHIND THE SALES PITCH

The truth was, Andy didn't want to tell lies anymore either. Claire was right. His missions presentation was like one of those sleek all-inclusive resorts on a tropical island, where tourists are pampered in luxury, while just outside the gate, people are starving. Andy had created a false picture of their life, and he was peddling it nearly every Sunday while they were on furlough.

In this Hollywood version of missionary life, Andy and Claire were happily homeschooling their kids while offering an "open door policy" to their neighbors in the community. They were in the midst of a project to dig a well for clean water, had recently begun sponsoring 10 children for school, and were sharing the good news of Jesus in weekly sessions at a popular gathering place in town. Life was good, the ministry was good, and the church partners were to thank (along with God, of course).

The reality was much worse, and not nearly as enticing. Claire was struggling to homeschool the kids, all three of whom seemed to have different learning styles. Moving from her corporate office job to homeschool mom was a much tougher transition than either of them had imagined. She had lost much of her identity, but struggled with guilt. As the seemingly happy moms around her so often reminded Claire, "Your identity is in Christ and your legacy is your children." Of course, that sounded great, but it didn't reflect Claire's inner reality.

The "open door policy" was more of a concession than a choice. Neighbors dropped by all the time - in the middle of school sessions, during meals, at the pinnacle of emotional breakdowns. It seemed that, for Andy and Claire's neighbors, any time of day was the right time of day for a visit. They recognized this as a cultural difference and decided they had no choice but to go along with it, but that didn't lessen the strain it put on their family.

The water well project was a disaster. What began with a desire to bring clean drinking water rushing to the surface had ended up sending a ton of money straight down the drain. Incompetent companies, corrupt officials, and a deep hole that simply didn't seem to want to give up any water had caused Andy and Claire to nearly walk away from missionary life completely. "Just one more shot," Andy had said. If the next attempt didn't work, they would abandon the project, with nothing to show for all their efforts.

The children Andy and Claire were sponsoring for school might become a success story one day. They clung to that hope. For now, though, the sponsorships were causing an added financial burden since a few large donors had dropped off.

Then there were those weekly sessions in town. The ones with only a hand full of people in attendance - drunks mostly - who came for the snacks.

Nothing was going well, and Andy and Claire wanted to give up. Their relationship had suffered immensely under the pressure, their kids felt the strain, their ministry was floundering, and their support was drying up just like that well. But the people who had sent them expected more of them. Their missions partners just loved the pictures of monkeys stealing their food, and they laughed at the stories of odd but well-intentioned gifts. They wanted to feel good about the work Andy and Claire were doing. They wanted the Hollywood version.

Missionaries, it seems, aren't allowed to fail. All things work together for good for those that love God. If it wasn't working, maybe it was Andy and Claire's fault. Maybe they didn't have enough faith or love God enough. Whatever the case, there was no way Andy could give an honest presentation. Nobody wanted to give money to something that wasn't working, and if nobody gave, they wouldn't be able to continue their work - to make any attempt to get back on track. So, he forged on with the lie. Hopefully, no one would attempt to peel back the facade.

And why should Andy feel he could be honest? His prior experience told him otherwise. When he had mentioned in a newsletter their lack of privacy from the neighbors, one friend responded with a diatribe about what a blessing it would be to have people who need Jesus literally coming to his door. When Claire had jokingly posted on her social media profile that she would rather poke herself in the eye than to try to teach her older kids about human anatomy, a family member decided to remind her that she had chosen this life and shouldn't complain about it.

The previous attempt to raise money for the water well had resulted in a long back and forth on their blog about why they couldn't just get another aid organization to dig the well (they had tried), why the people in their village couldn't just carry water (they did, 9.5 miles every day), and why digging a well was so much more expensive than in the U.S. (as if they had any control over that).

Andy wasn't honest because he really didn't think it would help. The expectation was for every project to succeed, for every dollar to multiply, and for the personal needs of Andy and his family to fade into the background as they "suffered for the cause of Christ."

RETHINKING OUR EXPECTATIONS

This is the dilemma faced by missionaries around the world on a daily basis. They are held to impossible standards, asked to do things they have no training or qualifications to do, and judged at every turn. Meanwhile, their families suffer without pastoral care while the church back home makes them poster children for "Global Challenge Sunday."

Is this the case for *every* missionary? Certainly not. Is it the case for *your* missionary partners and friends? I don't know, but it's a question worth asking.

What expectations, spoken or otherwise, have you placed on your missionary friends? Do you expect them to fit into your system or do you seek to understand the unique challenges and situations they face? Have you clarified what you expect from them, what they expect from you, and what both of you perceive the others' expectations to be?

Do you play the "one-up" game with your missionary friends? You know, "Oh, it's too bad you don't have power. My mom is sick in the hospital." Or, "I'm sorry that your staff member quit. My dishwasher broke, so I know how you feel."

Now is the time to clear the air with your missionary friends. (And, if you are a missionary, it's time to clear the air with your partners.) Let's talk about expectations and, where necessary, the lack thereof. Let's give each other permission to be human, to be held accountable when we fail, but to always be offered grace.

Let's give our missionary friends permission to not just

be the smiling face on the missions wall. We should be the ones encouraging them, rather than seeking validation of our meager missions support efforts. Yes, we all have problems, but generally, your missionary friend is not the person on whom to unleash your issues. Become a listener. Become a learner. Drop the expectations in exchange for an empathetic ear. What you receive in return could be the education of a lifetime.

CONCLUSION

IN A FEW INTENSE years, I've learned a lot about missionaries and their unusual lives. Their stories and my own experience living abroad have opened my eyes to the realities of this unique world.

My friend Christine gave me a lesson in purpose - finding hers in the education of young women in one of the world's harshest cities. My own first-hand experience revealed the impact short-term missions can have on the teams who go. Hundreds of missionary friends have taught me that the makeup of a missionary is as varied as the sands on the seashore, that home is a complex idea, and that the role of the sender is vital in the long-term success of the missionary.

On my journey to understand missions better, I also

discovered some of the more mundane aspects of missionary life. Louise taught me about the cost of doing missions. Tired and burnt out missionary friends reminded me of the value of local, personal pastoral care. The wild and weird world of underwater diving highlighted just how difficult it is to fully embrace new surroundings.

Over the years, I've also stumbled upon some unexpected discoveries, like the strange competition between missionaries and missions organizations and the unintended side-effects of missions work. I've felt the emotional sting of the complexities of communication, and have seen the anxiety and peril of the expectations game.

When considering all of these factors, my hope is that you have even more respect for your missionary friends. I pray you will consider how you could positively impact each of these areas for your missionary partners. Perhaps working backwards through this book, you could begin by altering your expectations, and improve your communications. Together, maybe missionaries and their partners can turn the tide of missionary life.

IT'S BAD, BUT NOT ALL BAD

When I set out to write this book, I knew I was undertaking a perilous task. I was hoping to enlighten non-missionaries to the realities of missionary life. In doing so, I knew I was treading on treacherous ground. Most missionaries I talk to have long ago given up on the idea that their friends, families, and supporters will ever come close to understanding their lives. Many are fearful of the backlash that would result from this type of honesty.

Some have determined to just smile and nod. Others have become hardened in very unhealthy ways. In the worst cases, they have thrown in the towel.

One missionary friend recently told me, "Nobody really cares what you're doing in ministry or how you're doing personally. They just like bragging to their friends that *they* are part of your ministry." Missionaries and their God-honoring work are being reduced to badges of honor for acolytes and socialites - disembodied symbols of humanitarianism and the Great Commission.

Perhaps that's a cynical view, but I think it is a stark reflection of the experience of many missionaries. They feel used by their partner churches, misunderstood by those who should be their greatest supporters, and abandoned by all but their closest friends.

This is where some cheerful missionary usually chimes in to let everyone know that this hasn't been their experience. To those missionaries, I would say, "You are the lucky ones." Perhaps their sending churches were better prepared than most. Perhaps the missionary and their partners are better at communication. Unfortunately, the majority of missionaries I talk to - now numbering in the hundreds - have experienced most or all of the struggles I've written about here.

Most of them will also tell you what a joy it is to serve God. They will tell you that the struggle is worth it. Some will even chastise me for writing from what they perceive to be a far too negative view of missions and missionary life. Nevertheless, the struggles I've written about here are real, and though you could argue that the end result is worth the battle, that doesn't mean we have to accept these challenges as status quo - that what is *normal* must necessarily become *normative*.

As missionaries and friends of missionaries, we have the ability to combat many of these issues. We have the tools to diffuse most of these situations. We do not have to be victims of current missions thinking. We can instead be reformers of the system.

DISCUSSIONS LONG OVERDUE

As I think back on the conversations that contributed to this book, I'm haunted by the fact that so many of these discussions should have happened long ago with someone other than me. To be sure, the missionary bears some responsibility and culpability in the matter. So often, it is the missionary who shies away from the difficult conversations - who hides behind the successes (or perceived successes) of their ministry, rather than addressing the difficulties they face personally and professionally.

However, I think it's time for our lot - the friends, family, supporters, and partners of missionaries - to own up to the fact that we simply haven't done our job over the decades. I know I haven't. As I said previously, I wrote this book, in part, to confess to my own inadequacy as a supporter and pastor of missionaries. My hope is that some of what I've learned through relationship with my missionary friends can help you as you reflect on your own missions efforts.

Missions, I've discovered, is like a giant magnifying glass. It magnifies our calling, our passions, and our reliance on God. It also magnifies our weaknesses, our insecurities, and our vulnerabilities. Relational strain is heightened. Spiritual attack is intensified. The delicate weave of emotional fabric is stretched, pulled, and torn.

The platitudes about suffering for Jesus and jewels in the crown can only take a person so far, especially when coming from those who can't hope to relate to the life of a missionary. No, what propels them forward is some strange mix of intestinal fortitude, spiritual dependence, and personal one-on-one support from committed friends, family, and pastors on the ground.

Missionaries, it turns out, aren't superheroes. Maybe it's time we stop expecting them to be. Perhaps we can allow them to take off the mask once and for all, and instead, celebrate them for who they are - ordinary people on an extraordinary mission from God!

TALK TO ME

To request an interview for
TV, RADIO, PRINT, BLOG, OR PODCAST,
visit
www.missionsunmasked.com/media

To book a *SPEAKING ENGAGEMENT,*
visit
www.missionsunmasked.com/booking

ABOUT THE AUTHOR

From the hills of East Tennessee to the Rift Valley in Kenya, Adam Mosley has had a life full of ups and downs. In ministry for nearly his entire adult life, Adam's current vocation is as the pastor of a multi-cultural, theologically-diverse, international church in Nakuru, Kenya - a church made up of people from over a dozen different nations and five continents. Adam is also an author, speaker, husband, and father of two incredible girls. He has a passion for seeing others live the life they are created to live, and for shining a light on the opportunities and challenges of missionary life.

OTHER BOOKS BY ADAM MOSLEY

The *EVERY DAY BIBLE* Series

The Every Day Bible series is written by an everyday guy to help everyday people enjoy the Bible every day. Each book is broken down into daily readings of just a few chapters each, accompanied by some "regular guy" observations.

Books in the EVERY DAY BIBLE Series include:

CPSIA information can be obtained
at www.ICGtesting.com
Printed in the USA
LVOW13s1003261216
518699LV00011B/937/P